RS18ILLUSTRATORS18ILLUSTRATORS18ILLUSTRATORS18ILLUSTRAT
S18ILLUSTRATORS18ILLUSTRATORS18ILLUSTRATORS18ILLUSTRATC
USTRATORS18ILLUSTRATORS18ILLUSTRATORS18ILLUSTRATORS18I
ORS18ILLUSTRATORS18ILLUSTRATORS18ILLUSTRATORS18ILLUSTRA
TRATORS18ILLUSTRATORS18ILLUSTRATORS18ILLUSTRATORS18ILL
RS18ILLUSTRATORS18ILLUSTRATORS18ILLUSTRATORS18ILLUSTRAT
S18ILLUSTRATORS18ILLUSTRATORS18ILLUSTRATORS18ILLUSTRATC
USTRATORS18ILLUSTRATORS18ILLUSTRATORS18ILLUSTRATORS18I
ORS18ILLUSTRATORS18ILLUSTRATORS18ILLUSTRATORS18ILLUSTRA
TRATORS18ILLUSTRATORS18ILLUSTRATORS18ILLUSTRATORS18ILL
RS18ILLUSTRATORS18ILLUSTRATORS18ILLUSTRATORS18ILLUSTRAT
S18ILLUSTRATORS18ILLUSTRATORS18ILLUSTRATORS18ILLUSTRATC
USTRATORS18ILLUSTRATORS18ILLUSTRATORS18ILLUSTRATORS18I
ORS18ILLUSTRATORS18ILLUSTRATORS18ILLUSTRATORS18ILLUSTRA
TRATORS18ILLUSTRATORS18ILLUSTRATORS18ILLUSTRATORS18ILL
RS18ILLUSTRATORS18ILLUSTRATORS18ILLUSTRATORS18ILLUSTRAT
S18ILLUSTRATORS18ILLUSTRATORS18ILLUSTRATORS18ILLUSTRATC
USTRATORS18ILLUSTRATORS18ILLUSTRATORS18ILLUSTRATORS18I
ORS18ILLUSTRATORS18ILLUSTRATORS18ILLUSTRATORS18ILLUSTRA
TRATORS18ILLUSTRATORS18ILLUSTRATORS18ILLUSTRATORS18ILL
RS18ILLUSTRATORS18ILLUSTRATORS18ILLUSTRATORS18ILLUSTRAT
S18ILLUSTRATORS18ILLUSTRATORS18ILLUSTRATORS18ILLUSTRATC
USTRATORS18ILLUSTRATORS18ILLUSTRATORS18ILLUSTRATORS18I
ORS18ILLUSTRATORS18ILLUSTRATORS18ILLUSTRATORS18ILLUSTRA
TRATORS18ILLUSTRATORS18ILLUSTRATORS18ILLUSTRATORS18ILL
RS18ILLUSTRATORS18ILLUSTRATORS18ILLUSTRATORS18ILLUSTRAT
S18ILLUSTRATORS18ILLUSTRATORS18ILLUSTRATORS18ILLUSTRATC
USTRATORS18ILLUSTRATORS18ILLUSTRATORS18ILLUSTRATORS18I
ORS18ILLUSTRATORS18ILLUSTRATORS18ILLUSTRATORS18ILLUSTRA
TRATORS18ILLUSTRATORS18ILLUSTRATORS18ILLUSTRATORS18ILL
RS18ILLUSTRATORS18ILLUSTRATORS18ILLUSTRATORS18ILLUSTRAT
S18ILLUSTRATORS18ILLUSTRATORS18ILLUSTRATORS18ILLUSTRATC
USTRATORS18ILLUSTRATORS18ILLUSTRATORS18ILLUSTRATORS18I
ORS18ILLUSTRATORS18ILLUSTRATORS18ILLUSTRATORS18ILLUSTRA
TRATORS18ILLUSTRATORS18ILLUSTRATORS18ILLUSTRATORS18ILL
RS18ILLUSTRATORS18ILLUSTRATORS18ILLUSTRATORS18ILLUSTRAT
S18ILLUSTRATORS18ILLUSTRATORS18ILLUSTRATORS18ILLUSTRATC
USTRATORS18ILLUSTRATORS18ILLUSTRATORS18ILLUSTRATORS18I
ORS18ILLUSTRATORS18ILLUSTRATORS18ILLUSTRATORS18ILLUSTRA
TRATORS18ILLUSTRATORS18ILLUSTRATORS18ILLUSTRATORS18ILL
RS18ILLUSTRATORS18ILLUSTRATORS18ILLUSTRATORS18ILLUSTRAT
S18ILLUSTRATORS18ILLUSTRATORS18ILLUSTRATORS18ILLUSTRATC
USTRATORS18ILLUSTRATORS18ILLUSTRATORS18ILLUSTRATORS18I
ORS18ILLUSTRATORS18ILLUSTRATORS18ILLUSTRATORS18ILLUSTRA
TRATORS18ILLUSTRATORS18ILLUSTRATORS18ILLUSTRATORS18ILL
RS18ILLUSTRATORS18ILLUSTRATORS18ILLUSTRATORS18ILLUSTRAT
S18ILLUSTRATORS18ILLUSTRATORS18ILLUSTRATORS18ILLUSTRATC
USTRATORS18ILLUSTRATORS18ILLUSTRATORS18ILLUSTRATORS18I
ORS18ILLUSTRATORS18ILLUSTRATORS18ILLUSTRATORS18ILLUSTRA
TRATORS18ILLUSTRATORS18ILLUSTRATORS18ILLUSTRATORS18ILL
RS18ILLUSTRATORS18ILLUSTRATORS18ILLUSTRATORS18ILLUSTRAT
S18ILLUSTRATORS18ILLUSTRATORS18ILLUSTRATORS18ILLUSTRATC
USTRATORS18ILLUSTRATORS18ILLUSTRATORS18ILLUSTRATORS18I
ORS18ILLUSTRATORS18ILLUSTRATORS18ILLUSTRATORS18ILLUSTR
TRATORS18ILLUSTRATORS18ILLUSTRATORS18ILLUSTRATORS18ILL
RS18ILLUSTRATORS18ILLUSTRATORS18ILLUSTRATORS18ILLUSTRA
S18ILLUSTRATORS18ILLUSTRATORS18ILLUSTRATORS18ILLUSTRAT
USTRATORS18ILLUSTRATORS18ILLUSTRATORS18ILLUSTRATORS18I
ORS18ILLUSTRATORS18ILLUSTRATORS18ILLUSTRATORS18ILLUSTR
TRATORS18ILLUSTRATORS18ILLUSTRATORS18ILLUSTRATORS18ILL
RS18ILLUSTRATORS18ILLUSTRATORS18ILLUSTRATORS18ILLUSTRA

# ILLUSTRATORS 18

THE EIGHTEENTH ANNUAL
NATIONAL EXHIBITION OF ILLUSTRATION
HELD IN THE GALLERIES OF
THE SOCIETY OF ILLUSTRATORS
128 EAST 63RD STREET, NEW YORK
FEBRUARY 11 THROUGH APRIL 15, 1976

# ILLUSTRATORS

# 18

NC
975
A1
I5
1976

THE EIGHTEENTH ANNUAL
OF AMERICAN ILLUSTRATION
PUBLISHED FOR THE SOCIETY OF ILLUSTRATORS
**HASTINGS HOUSE, PUBLISHERS, INC.**
NEW YORK 10016

# ILLUSTRATORS 18

**CONTENTS**

Officers of the Society of Illustrators

Annual Show Committee

Juries

The President's Message by Alvin J. Pimsler

The Chairman's Statement by Warren Rogers

Hall of Fame

   Winslow Homer by Charles McVicker

   Harvey Dunn by Steven R. Kidd

   John Falter by Stevan Dohanos

Hamilton King Award

   Judith Jampel by Jill Bossert

Point of View by Bob Heindel

An Attic Trunk of Anecdotes by Al Parker

Designer/Editor's Comments by Bob Hallock

The Exhibition

Index

Advertisements

ALVIN J. PIMSLER/SELF PORTRAIT

## ILLUSTRATORS 18 BY ALVIN J. PIMSLER, PRESIDENT

I think the Society of Illustrators performs one of its most valuable functions each year in putting together the Annual Exhibition of Illustration. Nowhere else is the best of all the facets of illustration gathered together for viewing by the artist, the art buyer, the art director, industry and the public.

For the artist it provides a forum for his point of view; enables him to see, in the original, the work of other illustrators, and keeps him stimulated and forward-looking.

For the art buyer, art director and industry, the exhibition offers the opportunity to see conveniently in one gallery how others have used illustration to their benefit, to examine the many and varied styles of different artists and to keep abreast of the developing trends in illustration.

The public often leaves the gallery with a new image of the work of illustrators in relation to its own concept of art.

## THE CHAIRMAN'S STATEMENT
## BY WARREN ROGERS

Everyone I spoke to led me to believe the chairman's job was horrendous, with a never-ending list of mishaps, arguments and generally a job no one would ever want.

My experience was quite the opposite. So many of the members were there to help when I needed it. The Society staff, Arpi's Army, are extraordinarily efficient, our struggles were minimal, and the 18th Annual Show is another winner.

My grateful thanks to all of you who submitted your work, and to all of you who contributed your time toward the show's success. I don't know how you all do it but you get better every year.

WARREN ROGERS BY JERRY McCONNELL

# HALL OF FAME

## WINSLOW HOMER
### BY CHARLES McVICKER

Winslow Homer's place in the Illustrators Hall of Fame is a reassurance to all artists who believe that illustration can be art and that the illustrator can also find a place in that elevated and sometimes elusive bastion called "fine art."

Born in Boston of old Yankee stock in 1836, Homer had his first art training as an apprentice to J. H. Bufford, a Boston lithographer. At the age of 21 he became a free-lance illustrator working mostly for *Harper's Weekly*. Two years later he moved to New York where he studied at the National Academy of Design and privately with Frederic Rondel. Becoming a staff artist for *Harper's* he did his most praised work as an illustrator during the Civil War, producing powerful drawings of the Union Army. He was an active illustrator for *Harper's* and other magazines and books until 1875.

Homer had begun painting in 1862. A hunter and fisherman, he loved the outdoor life. His early oils were illustrations of farm and summer resort scenes. They are authentic and direct. In 1873 he took up watercolor. On a trip to England in 1881 he began painting the sea and fishermen. In 1883 he settled in Prout's Neck, Maine, where he lived alone in a studio facing the sea. He painted the forest, hunters, fishermen, and a series of the greatest modern paintings of the sea. His summer visits to Cuba, Florida, Nassau and Bermuda resulted in brilliant and powerful watercolors and his most famous painting, "The Gulf Stream."

Winslow Homer died at Prout's Neck in 1910. Lloyd Goodrich of the Whitney Museum says of Winslow Homer: *His innocent eye, his direct recording of outdoor light and color, curiously parallel to his younger contemporaries, the French Impressionists, but without any possible influence from them, made him an indigenous forerunner of Impressionism. In maturity he became the greatest pictorial poet of outdoor America—the sea, the forest, the mountains, and the men who inhabited them. In his energy, the pristine freshness of his vision, and his simple sensuous vitality, he embodies the extrovert elements of the American spirit as no preceding artist had. His art was completely personal and native, with no discernible outside influences; while allied in a general way to Impressionism, it always retained the integrity of the object instead of dissolving it in luminous atmosphere.*

This direct approach to the subject in both his illustration and painting makes Homer the father of a strain of American illustration that persists to this day. Unadorned by intellectual manipulation this artistic viewpoint depicts our world in a clear-eyed, down-to-earth way that has great appeal to a large portion of the viewing public.

WINSLOW HOMER. "Dad's coming!" *Harper's Weekly, November 1, 1873*

# HALL OF FAME

HARVEY DUNN. *The American Legion Monthly*, January, 1928

## HARVEY DUNN BY STEVEN R. KIDD

My heart leapt with joy when Willis Pyle asked me to talk on Harvey Dunn's election to the Hall of Fame. It is a signal honor to speak on Mr. Dunn's behalf.

As Marc Connolly wrote in "Green Pastures"—"PUT OUT *ALL* DE LIGHTS! AND CALL DE LAWD! *RIGHT NOW!*

Mr. Dunn had a favorite quote from the Bible—Paul's Epistle to the Philippians: "Whatsoever things be true, honest, just, pure, lovely or of good report, if there be any virtue, or any praise, think on these things." (Don't think *about* them.)

Harvey Dunn's election to the Hall of Fame is a recognition of the profound legacy left by this giant in illustration. The most powerful painter/illustrator of the first half of this century, a magnificent life force, transcendental thinker and great teacher, aware of the brotherhood of man, said, "The only thing true about *you* is your spirit."

Through him, students had a direct line to the great painters of the past.

The unity of design and idea, the quality of resonance in his tonal arrangements, were as played upon a mighty organ. He said, there are *big* ideas, and *little* ideas, and if you can't be powerful, be charming; to all ideas he was a gracious host. With poetic perception that pierced beyond the facts, he dealt with the epic.

LISTEN! LISTEN! The starry skies and hills are singing, the morning dew glistens on the prairie, and the wind blows the grass—light is everywhere—for where no light enters, *there* is darkness.

It was a blessed experience to have known Harvey Dunn —and to his name be all *glory, majesty* and praise.

JOHN FALTER. Gramercy Park. *The Saturday Evening Post*, March 25, 1944

## JOHN FALTER BY STEVAN DOHANOS

John Falter's Credo, in his own words: "It has been my hope to record what is probably the last of the great tradition of farming, of river life, of the domestic life so closely related to it, and of the small bits of peace and serenity that only exist close to nature.

"In treating what is, to me, a profoundly appealing subject, I have tried to be completely impersonal; it has been my wish to observe and record, to document and to commend the poetic way of life I have observed in many parts of America, from the Amish men of Pennsylvania to the cat fishermen of the Missouri River."

Let's retrace his steps. Let's go back and see how he started.

In 1910, John was born at the mouth of the great Platt River in Plattsmouth, Nebraska.

Raised in Falls City, he inherited a pioneer quality of Big Spaces, of Big Skies and of Big Rivers.

In Falls City his father ran a men's clothing store (this year celebrating its 60th anniversary).

John's first earnings bought him a saxophone.

He did not know, at that time, that he would eventually sketch and paint from life 40 greats of jazz including Louis Armstrong, Jack Teagarden, Pee Wee Russell, Jeff Johnson and many others.

John didn't make it as a musician. Obviously, he was destined to make it as an artist, instead.

But he did play in a band of sorts.

We all remember the "Loud Sounds," an informal group of artists and art directors. They gathered together at the Society on many occasions. Regulars included: Al Parker, Ken Thompson, Dick Lockwood, Paul Smith, Cliff Sterratt, Clark Agnew and Falter, of course.

In 1928 he enrolled as a student at Kansas City Art Institute.

Then he won a scholarship to the Art Students League in New York and studied with Frank Bridgeman.

After the League, from 1930 to 1940, he was a successful illustrator of fiction and worked on some great advertising accounts. (He made a tremendous impact with a series for Pall Mall cigarettes.)

He entered the Navy in 1943; commissioned a Lieutenant on special art assignments. He did more than 300 recruiting pamphlets and posters.

While in the Navy he also did a notable series of 12 portraits of Great War Heroes, with text by Paul Gallico. These were published as *Esquire* gatefolds. On the reverse were pinups of Petty and Varga girls. As a result, Falter had most of his work turned to the wall.

In 1944, "Gramercy Park" (illustrated), his first *Saturday Evening Post* cover, appeared — a painting he had done for pleasure. From then on, until the *Post* ceased publication in the early 60s, John produced 175 covers.

My impression of Falter's *Post* period, as a fellow contributor, was that they were monthly installments of his Credo above.

Most notable was his series of famous streets of great cities: Park Avenue, Peachtree Street, Michigan Boulevard etc.

One great cover depicted Truman addressing the House and Senate — a fabulous tableau of recognizable members.

John also toured and painted the Pennsylvania Dutch country, depicting the Amish farmers and their lives.

In the 50s, while living in San Francisco, he studied the Flemish painting techniques with Henry Rusk, the conservator of the DeYoung Museum and the Palace of the Legion of Honor. Though he continued his editorial and advertising work, he began to paint more and more for his own pleasure. He has done many portraits all through these years — including major portraits of Olivia de Haviland, Mrs. Clark Clifford, Dorothy Stickney, James Cagney, John Charles Thomas, Admiral Halsey and the 40 lithographs of the jazz greats.

In the 60s, he did less and less commercial work, concentrating on book illustration and private commissions.

From 1968 to 1970, he researched the Santa Fe and Oregon Trails, a trip his grandparents had made in a covered wagon.

And in the 70s he did a series of six Bicentennial paintings for Minnesota Mining & Manufacturing Co. (the 3M company.)

He recently completed designs for two U.S. Postage stamps — the subject: "Rural America." Featured were the Chautauqua Tent in one; Kansas wheat fields in the other. He has, therefore, come full circle.

We know that: John did not go into his father's business; John did not make Big Time Jazz; John did not personally win World War II. *But*, he had a lot to say about America with paint and brush.

It is now our time to recognize his outstanding contribution to American illustration.

# HAMILTON KING AWARD

## JUDITH JAMPEL BY JILL BOSSERT

The Society of Illustrators is proud to present this year's Hamilton King Award to Judith Jampel for her wonderfully expressive "soft sculpture" of Bella Abzug, an unpublished piece done for Steve Phillips of *New Times* Magazine.

Born in London, England, in 1944, Judith was raised in New York City, where she later attended Hunter College studying archaeology. In 1966 she switched her major to art and studied at the School of Visual Arts, where she received an in-resident scholarship for 1967-68. Her art training also includes courses at Parsons School of Design.

Ms. Jampel began her career as a designer, during which time she received many awards; among them: *Creativity '71, '73* from *AD* Magazine; Andy Award 1972; TDC 19 Award; AIGA Communication Graphics 1972-73. Though she continued drawing during her stint as a designer, she began mastering her distinctive three-dimensional style in 1973.

The basic form of her soft creations are handsewn from nylon and polyester with skillful addition of fabric, hair and appropriate buttons, medals and bows. These figures are carefully articulated and have the fascinating ability to change expression at the artist's discretion.

Since she began her particular craft, Ms. Jampel has been represented in the Society of Illustrators 15, 17, as well as the 18th Annual Shows, receiving an Award for Excellence in Illustrators 17 for her timely Sam Ervin piece. She has also exhibited in the Greengrass Media Art Gallery and is appearing in the Society's *Library of American Illustration*, Three-Dimensional volume. Currently her clients include Ballantine Books, *New Times* Magazine, *Penthouse*, *Viva*, *Fortune*, *New York Times* Op-Ed page and *Emergency Medicine*.

Though caricatures of a kind, the Jampel figures are not cartoons. There is a cynical and almost eerie aspect about them due, in part, to the uncanny likeness of the subject portrayed. More striking, however, is the unsettling quality they possess that makes them just this side of living.

BELLA ABZUG BY JUDITH JAMPEL

BOB HEINDEL BY JOHN COLLIER

## POINT OF VIEW BY BOB HEINDEL

It would seem that this business of making pictures has remained fairly constant over the years. Styles manage only to repeat themselves. Because, no matter how hard we try to avoid it, and regardless of the words we attach to *ism*—whether it be *surreal* or *impression*—for the illustrator it always comes down to *real*.

Whatever changes have occurred are merely reflections of society in general. A little more sex and violence; a lot less mom and apple pie. As documented in this Annual, we are in the business of showing the world what it's about. We all like to believe we're marching to a different drum, when, in point of fact, we just stumble differently.

The really bright spot in our business appears to be in viewpoint. Whether we like it or not, we are more and more called upon to have one. This would seem to represent a kind of freedom that was much less visible before the photographic onslaught of a decade ago. As exciting as this freedom might be, it is hotly pursued by a creature called responsibility—in part to one's client, but mostly to one's self.

This condition has had a rather interesting side effect. We appear to be much less the stepchild of "fine art," while, at the same time, the "fine artist" has become the consummate "commercial artist." The merits and shortcomings of this I'll leave to more learned souls than myself to debate.

If one had listened to, and believed, all of the dialogue about this business 10 or 15 years ago, we would not exist today. I'm sure that the concerns were real then, and they continue to be. We certainly have an ample supply of problems, and not so many easy solutions. However, I would guess that as long as the world needs a mirror, we'll have a market.

No matter. The business of making pictures is generally a pleasure—always frustrating to a degree, and sometimes wonderfully rewarding.

When viewed against the background of problems that face mankind, what we do is so relatively meaningless that we might as well try to be extraordinary.

AL PARKER BY DICK COLE

## AN ATTIC TRUNK OF ANECDOTES

## WORDS AND MUSIC BY AL PARKER

He strode into the classroom homburg in hand. "Good afternoon," he said, removing a houndstooth topcoat from his shoulders. Never once did he wear his arms in the sleeves. Such *panache!* The hat and coat were always placed on the plaster-cast Venus by the door, one of the wall-to-wall statuary used as models for charcoal studies in the mornings. This charismatic gentleman was our instructor, Harlan Frazer, the illustrator admired by everyone, especially Evelyn and me. Evelyn was the teenager whose easel stood at my right. We had just met and already I had shared her brown-bag lunch and canvas stretching—oil paint was the medium in 1924. She was brushing boldly away on a portrait of Don Quixote as I painted a full length Fu Manchu. Mr. Frazer gave us the most interesting assignments. He also foretold my future: "I'll see your name in lights." Well, I failed to make it on a marquee, although I came close by playing a role in the school's performance of "It Pays to Advertise," and once my name appeared on an outdoor billboard in Phoenix in letters taller than I. How-

ever, it was Evelyn who won a scholarship to the Art Students League in New York, causing me to forsake credence in Mr. Frazer's prediction.

At that time there were no credits, degrees or a graduation at the St. Louis School of Fine Arts of Washington University. Students simply quit when they had enough. The tuition was approximately $37.50 a semester. After four years we had enough. Many many years later our good friend Bernie Fuchs attended the same school. Too late and too bad, for he plays trumpet and would have been an asset to our band. Evelyn canceled her scholarship rather than romance by mail. Parting was unthinkable—and still is.

### THE CAPTAIN SPEAKS

I was paying my way through art school by blowing a C-melody saxophone working the Mississippi riverboats, country clubs, college proms, Polish weddings and Dime-a-Dance halls. Grandpa, (Captain Charles J. Bender) for want of something to do during his retirement, took on my career as a project by donating my first year's tuition to art school. He was on board the *Robert E. Lee* when she won that famous race with the *Natchez*. Later, as captain on the *James Lee*, he graciously let Mark Twain sit at his table and also let him take over on the pilot wheel for kicks. Bullhorns had not yet replaced megaphones. Grandpa couldn't care less. He bellowed without either, and bellow he did while expressing his disapproval of my musical bent.

The first morning as I left for school he bellowed: "Beware of those Barbara La Marr types with their greasy eyelids and tweezed eyebrows," probably referring to the naked models which I was to find not as beautiful as Miss La Marr by far. Most rivermen set both moral and immoral standards depending on the quality of female passengers available on any given trip. Mom told me that, in hushed tones.

Upon leaving school I immediately became employed by a commercial art studio. My cockiness soon waned with the onslaught of fast-fast demands on my green-green talent. The studio's strange practice of signing its name to my efforts brought a frustrating tag of anonymity. Yet, in retrospect, it was a blessing, for it impelled its excellent lettering man and designer, Russell Viehman, and me to establish a studio on our own limited funds. No lawyers, just faith. We accepted any job our "rep," Frances Deppe, brought through the door —on which was lettered THE ILLUSTRATORS. The artwork ran the gamut from a drybrush sketch of Niagara Falls to a cluster of cold tablets on the palm of a hand. What a far cry from Fu Manchu in glorious color!

### FRONTAL NUDITY

What would have happened should Miss Frances have asked us to illustrate a "how to" book with frontal nudity? In the first place, despite the "Roaring Twenties" and its "Jazz Age" of "Flaming Youth," the decorum of the day would have forbidden such an endeavor before it left the fantasy stage; secondly, folks back home could wing it without benefit of diagrammatic pictorializing. Yesterday's Victorian discipline also forbade use of four-letter words in the presence of ladies. Only once did I break that unwritten rule in our studio, saying "shit" when I cut off the tip of my thumb with a mat knife. I repeat it here, not for updating this piece with a contemporary flavor, but to indicate in context how prettiness prevailed, and warts and all were a no-no.

I had only one confrontation with censorship; it dealt with rear nudity. My watercolor was a back view of a nude for the *Ladies Home Journal* in a 14th-century setting. A carved wood chair covered her *derriere*, a delightful contrast of fretwork against her flesh. It was censored on sight. I compromised by upholstering the chair. Later, when the illustration appeared, *Esquire* magazine, then in trouble over some censored art, used my nude as an example of the perversion that was allowed to penetrate the women's magazines. "A tempest in a molehill," I complained. The *Daily News* headlined "THE JOURNAL IS NO LADY." The court's judge cleared the air in stating that it was the caption under the illustration that was lewd, not my artwork. I paraphrase the caption: "Releasing the ribbons at her shoulders, the nightgown fell to the floor." Writers were permitted the bottom line in matters of soft-core sex that hinted of prurient titillations—even consenting adultery was closeted in the text of magazines! Illustrations told another story with fig leaves over the warts, figuratively speaking. But they did reflect the times—to a degree.

## THE EGG AND US
Evelyn and I were wed. Excitement reigned, toasting a new studio and our delightful new $75 a month apartment in Clayton, just outside St. Louis. We furnished it in "Art Moderne," the decor of the day. Life looked up, but only briefly. Wall Street seized the moment to lay its famous egg, causing the distemper of the times as well as the disintegration of our biggest client—the cold tablet company that never paid us the money we had already spent. Adversities corroded our innocent young lives along with all of the U.S.A. Hope returned somewhat when the service magazine *House Beautiful* held a cover contest. I entered and won $250. The better with the bitter.

Exactly nine months and fifteen minutes later our first son, Jay, was born. Trapped in the great depression with the resultant retrenchments meant leaving the luxury of our apartment for a newly-built cottage in nearby Overland, Missouri at $35 per month rental. With a third mouth to feed and few local jobs in sight, I chose to make contacts in the East.

Saving model fees, I posed Ev, Frances and our cornet player's girl friend, dashing off three heads rendered in colored pencils. Mailed them to the wonderful representative, Celia Mendelsohn, in New York. She promptly sold them to Frank Eltonhead, art editor of *Ladies Home Journal*, to grace its beauty pages. "Too far out" or, as they said, "too bizarre" for fiction pages.

The fashion editor was impressed and forwarded garden party dresses to be rendered in the same technique. I never fancied myself a fashion artist; however, with the kind assistance of Janet Lane, I became one. She was a true fashion artist who rented space from us. She usually worked hidden behind *frou-frou* furbelows and garments on hangers borrowed from the department store, Stix, Baer and Fuller.

I learned radical anatomy from her: figures eight heads tall and what happens to hemlines under certain conditions—all the tricks of her trade. I was not adverse to aid in pulling up my bootstraps.

## THE $1000 MISCONNECTION
Should you think this is a yawn-inducing blow-by-blow account of my life story, forget it. My *raison d'être* is to deliver a few anecdotes, some short, some long, all of them true, of an illustrator's existence way back—as today's students say—way back in those camp, funky days when the earth was flat.

Models, props, backgrounds all were painted from life. Not unlike the French with their *pochades*. Of course, we resorted to scrap on the unavailable—such as Washington crossing the Delaware. Once I needed to sketch in pencil a farmer's harvesting machine parked outdoors by a barn. It was 15° below zero and my brown mustache was white with frost. My gloves created tonal qualities where none were intended. In the summer, more than once, the thermometer rose to 120° as we labored in our underwear—the girls in kimonos. Air conditioning was in the planning stage. Meeting deadlines was hazardous to your health.

My very first manuscript arrived from *Woman's Home Companion*. Their art editor, Henry Quinan, saw more in those fashion jobs than I believed existed. After a month of false starts, the job flew to New York. While sitting on the sill of our open window, I read his telegram: "Congratulations—stop—am sending check for $1000." I almost fell the 12 floors to Locust Street. But the next morning he phoned: "Our editors disagree with me because you are unknown; am forwarding check for $400. When are you coming East?" Having just dropped $600 overnight, I became tongue-tied and mumbled something like "no plans."

Five years later when we met, he said, "You are not the taciturn chappie (he was English) I thought you were," cupping his hand to his ear as I jabbered away in my Midwestern twang.

## FROGGY, FROGGY DEW
Charlie Eubanks, our band's drummer, combined our surnames into THE PARBANKS SOCIETY ORCHESTRA. We played all over the area and spent time off watching Bix Beiderbecke blow cornet at the Arcadia Ballroom and Louis Armstrong on the riverboat *Capitol*. One special night, it was Glen Gray and his Casa Loma Orchestra, the most innovative big band of them all, on leave from the Essex House in New York for one night gigs in the Middle West. They were appearing in a nearby town in Illinois, noted as a gangster hideaway.

It was starting to drizzle as Charlie adjusted the isinglass sides at the windows of his phaeton, a pea-green model A with orange wire wheels (that was the year Ford discovered color). Evelyn and I piled into the car, our raincoats hiding the fact we had stepped out of a Floyd M. Davis illustration, wearing sleek clothes only Davis could have selected for his chic people with heavy-lidded eyes—those burnt holes in a blanket that gazed in complete boredom from magazines everywhere—idols to emulate. It drizzled into a raging storm, saturating the countryside. "It's fuzzy hail," said Evelyn in disbelief, squinting to see what the fuzz was that peppered the hood. However, the wipers kept sweeping away, not "fuzzy hail" but real live tiny *frogs*. It was raining *frogs*!

We entered the hall during an intermission. Pee Wee Hunt, Gray's trombone man, stood talking by the doorway. "Where's everybody?" The storm had abated, but too late to fill the hall with dancers. I told him of our unbelievable experience. "I don't know what you guys are drinkin' down here, but it sure is fierce stuff." We were cold sober. Prohibition was in effect. One couldn't trust a bootlegger in *this* town. To drive with a bottle of hootch in the car was foolhardy indeed.

A Robert Ripley "Believe It or Not" cartoon, read by 80 million people in 38 countries, verified the phenomenon we had witnessed with the frogs. Pee Wee never recalled the fact when I showed him the clipping a few years later.

## TREE ON THE ROOF

Curious to see the art editor with whom I had been working the past four years, I boarded a Ford tri-motored plane that rattled to New York in 23 hours from St. Louis. Accompanying me was Phil Davis, cartoonist on "Mandrake the Magician," who rented space in our studio. My friend, Lee Falk, writer of the strip, first offered it to me, but I was already a dedicated illustrator.

Seeing New York City from the air, with the only tree in sight on a roof, flabbergasted me. Phil said, "Pretend you're a New Yorker and don't ogle." He was so cool.

At the Society of Illustrators that night, I met the great artists in person. The large size of their original art on the walls was surprising. My water colors were actual repro size or a quarter up. A dubious asset, for some art directors hesitated paying so much for so little. At the evening's end I floated with euphoria to 26th Street before catching a cab to my hotel. (The Society was on West 24th Street in 1935.)

I bought a double-breasted gray flannel suit, tucked a blue cornflower in its lapel, caught a crosstown trolley on 59th Street to sightsee. Passing the St. Moritz Hotel, I saw a sight: Phil having tea at the sidewalk cafe. "Hi, Phil!" I shouted from the trolley above the traffic's din. "How ya doin'?" He barely flinched, his eyes darted left and right over the brim of his teacup as if to locate the Phil I was greeting. New York was another way of life.

## THE SCREAMING SWASTIKA

After giving Russell, my former studio partner, the stack of *National Geographic* we had shared, and after tearful farewells to our parents, Ev, Jay and I moved to the Big Apple. Our overhead skyrocketed—$250 for a 20th floor apartment on Central Park West, $50 for the garage, and $125 a month for illustrator Henry Raleigh's old studio in the Hotel des Artistes. Working long hours at the source, sometimes around the clock, I amassed enough cash to afford a vacation in Europe—before it was destroyed. War rumblings were becoming constant. We booked passage on the Dutch ship *Rotterdam* to loll a week doing

nothing. She was midway across the Atlantic when we bolted upright at the sight overhead. A Nazi flag was run up the mast. Its swastika seemed to scream "Achtung!" Germany had taken over the Holland Line as we were sunning ourselves on deck. Arriving safely in Southampton, shaken and staggering with sea legs, we headed for London, rented a car in Piccadilly Circus, and with Evelyn's elbow nudging *keep left*, *keep left*, we drove to Cliveden.

In that time, illustrators received mounds of fan mail. Our *rapport* with readers was to last longer than our art work. One such letter came from Joyce Grenfell, a young niece of Lady Astor. She had invited us to visit should we ever be in England. (Years later she became a famous actress of stage and screen.) Aside from losing my passport, we had a grand time together. She found it the next day behind a settee, where it had slid from my jacket as she sewed a loosened button back in place. Once I lost my passport in Monte Carlo. I'm a good loser.

Parisians were singing in the streets as we arrived. A double celebration of Bastille Day and Expo '37. We joined in the festivities, gorging on food, fun, Pernod, black cigars, the Louvre, Petit Palais and Picasso.

When armed guards appeared by our hotel doorway and French soldiers began to appear from nowhere, we booked passage on the *Normandie* for a quick trip home.

## BY A BABBLING BROOK

New York was deserted. It was August. It was hot. Jay found wearing white shoes down the elevator for supervised play in Central Park not to his liking. Ev missed her cactus collection, and I wanted a place to work without distractions.

Driving up the Post Road (no parkways) we found it —a colonial house by a babbling brook. We rented and began decorating with paint and wallpaper. The landlord was most appreciative, proudly putting the house up for sale. Mother Nature fortunately cancelled his plans with a bang. Wind and rain of tremendous proportions battered Larchmont and the Eastern seaboard. A willow tree, roots and all, flew past our living room window leaving a crater the size of a swimming pool.

We had been involved with tornadoes in St. Louis where you hid below ground. Seeking refuge in the basement, we found that the brook had beaten us there. Floating about aimlessly was an old kitchen table, Ev's jars of jam huddled on top, like derelicts on a raft. We identified with the jam.

## LATE, LATE SHOW

Hurricanes were temporarily forgotten. Our daughter, Susan, was born. I discarded my saxophone with its homespun sound and bought a set of drums. (It was at this time that I began painting mother and daughter covers for *Ladies Home Journal*—an assignment that was to continue for 13 years.)

Now a darkroom was needed. Model fees had climbed to $10 an hour—hence the need of photographs to work by. Arthur William Brown had used them all along, rather quietly, for such a crutch was frowned upon in our artistic circles. Not by me. Anything that helped produce an effective illustration was a legitimate tool. Back in St. Louis I had raised eyebrows when I used an air brush and a pantograph.

Social life in the East was as formidable as the work schedule. Editors and art directors combined business with the pleasure of our company. Cordial relationships developed into steadfast friendships. Luncheons, cocktail parties and dinners were given for their illustrators, where one could hobnob with other contributors, celebrities, and VIPs from Eleanor Roosevelt to Humphrey Bogart (whose mother was an illustrator).

The brilliant editor, Herbert R. Mayes, introduced us to a young and shy Andy Warhol, a newcomer in high-laced shoes. "He bears watching," said Herb, who always picked talent before it ripened. Herb also raised illustrators' fees to $2500 per job. He even got an author to write a story based on an illustration I made up!

Those times acquired a late, late show character.

We went nightclubbing, part of the carriage trade in white tie and tails. I still have the collapsible top hat. To cavort in madcap adventures was our Saturday night special. One editor chartered a Fifth Avenue bus for a roving cocktail party, drinking and dancing to an accordion as we traveled about the side streets. The natives were wide-eyed in astonishment. Exotic *hors d'oeuvres* caused some consternation. What appeared to be crinkled cereal, and smelled of being marinated in kerosene, was actually dried grasshoppers, grubs, and assorted insects that popped, snapped and crackled as I nibbled away, refusing to reveal shock at the host's gag. I assumed a cloak of suavity as undaunted as a David Niven.

## CORNFIELDS AND CRICKETS

Larchmont's proximity to New York meant easy shuttling, no longer the ideal hideaway. Connecticut, with cornfields and crickets, beckoned. We envisaged a house high on a hill with nary a brook in sight. A studio and darkroom would be attached, all by a cornfield, of course. We found it in Westport, where we remained for 15 years, scheduling three illustrations a month.

So the dream came true up to the shock of the bombing of Pearl Harbor, which put finis to the late, late show, epicurean delights and zany escapades.

Only the Society of Illustrators jazz group was to remain—a sextet formed of musician-artists who played for the Society's events, television, radio and hospitalized servicemen. We had a ball, especially the afternoon Benny Goodman sat in with us. And the time Buddy Rich and I had a duet—whereby he demolished my ego with dispatch. Ken Thompson, our piano man, composed our theme song "63rd Street Sorrow Blues." The melody varied depending on our mood—but always in the key of C, for Ken was allergic to lots of sharps and flats.

War shortages abounded. Art supplies such as English Whatman board, so favored by illustrators, were the first to vanish. We discovered gesso panels were a superb replacement. Its new surface suggested new techniques. Make-do persevered. Gasoline had no substitute and was rationed at three gallons a week. Illustration wasn't recognized as a necessary occupation. Rationed scarcities varied geographically. Russell, back home in St. Louis, was allotted more gas for his powermower than I received in a month for the Lincoln Zephyr. Our third child, son Kit, was born.

## SKY RIDERS

We were having lunch together in a small sandwich shop on a quiet street in Westport with Marilyn Monroe, her manager, my friend and excellent photographer, Milton Greene, his wife Amy, Ev and me—Marilyn attired in halter top and shorts that revealed an absolutely flawless skin touched pink from sunshine. She was without makeup—no evidence of a movie sex goddess. Her unaffected naturalness was refreshing.

Ev and I dropped a bombshell on the conversation by mentioning our plans to leave for the West. Westport had replaced cornfields with houses. Progress had gone too far. And, too, we had lived in the East for 20 years. It was time to change the scene. Marilyn exhorted on pitfalls out West. Later I was to encounter one of them in Hollywood with Marilyn and Sir Laurence Olivier.

Arizona was our first stop. Our friends, illustrator Robert G. Harris and family, had left Westport earlier and loved Scottsdale. We rented there, locating my studio at the nearby Phoenix airport in the Sky Riders Hotel. I was knee deep in American Airlines' ad art, ergo that appropriate setting. Outside the studio was a palm-lined swimming pool which provided the necessary pilots and stewardesses as models. Lawrence Drake, who had supplanted Celia Mendelsohn when we had arrived in New York years ago, was along. It was business as usual irrespective of the vacation atmosphere.

While there, we met the award-winning cartoonist Gus "Gordo" Arriola and his wife, Fran. We were old friends from the start. When he was incapacitated with a back injury, and unable to work, I gladly volunteered to do his strip. In the process, I learned of the cartoonist's arduous schedule, a work-a-day world of incessant chuckles. To imitate his masterly performance was impossible; however, my efforts did deceive his fans as I labored mightily those pinch-hitting weeks—a most enjoyable interlude even so.

## I SLEPT IN MARILYN'S BED

A poster assignment took me to Hollywood. After posing Natalie Wood and Tab Hunter, I phoned Milt and Amy Greene in Beverly Hills to say hello. They invited me to dinner. We had fun talking about Westport days, and they suggested I stay over in their guest room, now Marilyn's bedroom. She was hospitalized with a strep throat, contracted while filming "Bus Stop."

It was a charming French Provincial room. Marilyn's difficulty in sleeping demanded the shutting out of all light and sound. The only suggestion of female occupancy was the usual array of cosmetics. A gilt frame on the night table had a snapshot of an elderly man sitting in a reed rocker on a Victorian porch with a small dog curled up at his feet. I was never to hear the story behind the photo, but, whoever he might be, his comforting presence must have been close to her heart. I felt like an intruder, but slept in her bed anyway.

Later on, a billboard poster was decided upon for Marilyn in "The Sleeping Prince." I suggested for the symbol a white Graustarkian boot complete with golden spur, lying across the poster, with Marilyn's head and shoulders with her half-exposed breasts about to pop out of the boot. She loved the idea and all was serene until Sr. Laurence Olivier was chosen as co-star and the title changed to "The Prince and the Showgirl." Gradually the poster became a travesty of its original intent. Came the hassle of whose head was in front, the placement and size of their names, the myriad of movie laws peculiar to posters necessitating time-consuming solutions and a final compromise that set me uptight. I swore off show business for good. There was plenty of fiction available to illustrate and a boom in advertising art to make me forget Hollywood. But not winsome M.M.

## BRING ON THE ENCOMIUMS

Scottsdale offered not only grandeur and majestic saguero cactus, but also rattlesnakes, scorpions and dust devils. The wanderlusting Arriolas and Parkers moved to Carmel Valley, California where we remain ensconced these past 20 years. It is not as isolated as one might think.

Recently my contacts with art students have been heartwarming indeed. Some from the University of Utah chartered a bus for a coastal trip, dropping by my home to spend an afternoon of questions, answers and general studio talk. The giant Greyhound bus parked in our driveway dwarfed everything in sight. Our black cat, Rosebud, left for days.

A retrospective exhibition of my work, at San Francisco's Academy of Art College, brought forth students wearing T-shirts on which was printed a likeness of my face and signature—designed by friend Dick Cole. I was overwhelmed. It's nice to receive encomiums while you're still alive.

## BREAD

Illustrators' gratuitous lecture trips made one a bonafide docent as we traveled all over the United States and Canada, from Montreal to San Diego, from Miami to Vancouver, and all major stops in between, speaking by request before art organizations and schools. Both the giving and receiving of fresh viewpoints, not visible in the confines of a studio, brought much enlightenment from these exchanges.

Illustrators working in the genre of the times were in the $10,000 or so a month bracket, not including the perquisite from sales of second rights to magazines overseas. The low cost of living presented an additional dividend. Lacking was the inflation of today with prices that soar into the stratosphere.

I understand that today's illustrators are paid less for their efforts, though they have a more flexible market and freedom. Other professions seem to have kept their bread abreast of the times. What a shame. Justice has sold out to a kangaroo court.

Time to leave space in this *Annual 18* for Bob Hallock's linkage of images and text, and to salute his magnum opus, *Lithopinion*, which was an inspiration for over a decade— *a memoire extraordinaire!*

BOB HALLOCK BY BERNIE FUCHS

## DESIGNER/EDITOR'S COMMENTS
BY BOB HALLOCK

In 1959 I designed the First Annual Exhibition book for the Society of Illustrators. It showed the 311 illustrations in that show. This year's book contains 501 examples. Exhibited in two sections—Editorial and Book from February 11-March 9; Advertising, Institutional and TV/Film from March 17-April 15, 1976, it filled the SI galleries with glowing color and texture. This book can only attempt to be a record and can't capture the physical presence of the show. But illustration's primary purpose is to be reproduced. I have attempted to be fair to all exhibitors. It is a formidable job of organization by everyone involved. Thanks to them all for a vital roundup.

Use of color was contingent upon availability of film separations from the sources. Originally 150 were requested, but only 85 were possible to obtain. These are shown at the same size as originally run. All black-and-white illustrations are from 8 x 10 photographs.

I especially want to thank Al Parker and Bob Heindel for their comments as illustrators representing respectively "the good old days" and today. Al Parker was long the pacesetter when magazines were big and fat. He left Westport, Connecticut, a number of years ago and lives in Carmel Valley, California. Bob Heindel lives and works in Fairfield, Connecticut. They both represent the finest tradition of illustration.

**1**
*Editorial*
Artist: **Richard Sparks**
Art Director: Burton Pollack
Publication: Patient Care
**Gold Medal**

**2**
*Editorial*
Artist: **David Palladini**
Art Director: Harry Costas Coulianos
Publication: Gentlemen's Quarterly

**3**
*Advertising*
Artist: **Jeffrey A. Schrier**
Art Director: Jeffrey A. Schrier

**4**
*Institutional*
Artist: **Bernard Fuchs**
Art Director: Jim Bonner
Agency: Jim Bonner Adv. Art
Client: West-Port-Orleans, Ltd.

**5**
*Institutional*
Artist: **Bernard Fuchs**
Art Director: Jim Bonner
Agency: Jim Bonner Adv. Art
Client: West-Port-Orleans, Ltd.

**6**
*Advertising*
Artist: **Paul Giovanopoulos**
Art Director: Ron Vareltzis
Client: Geigy Pharmaceuticals

**7**
*Institutional*
Artist: **Reagan Wilson**
Art Director: Reagan Wilson

**8**
*Book*
Artist: **Robert Heindel**
Art Director: Gordon Fisher
Title: The Grapes of Wrath
Publisher: The Franklin Library

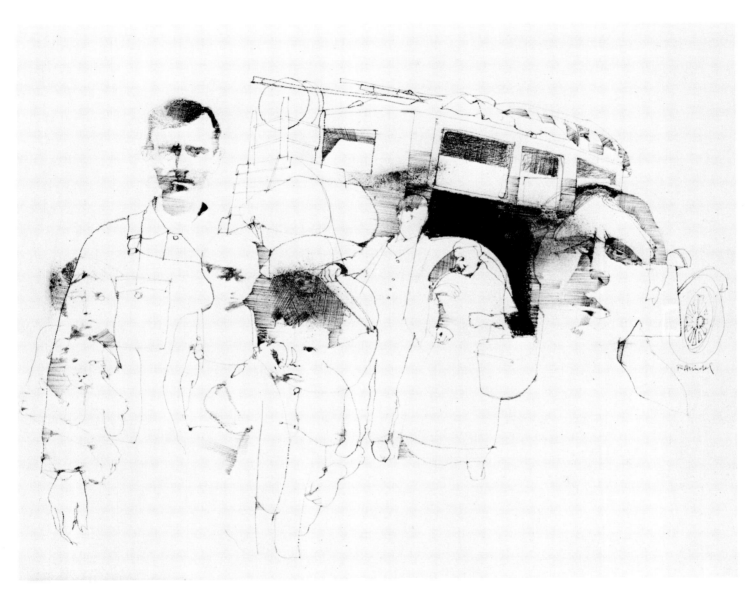

**9**
*Book*
Artist: **Robert Heindel**
Art Director: Gordon Fisher
Title: The Grapes of Wrath
Publisher: The Franklin Library

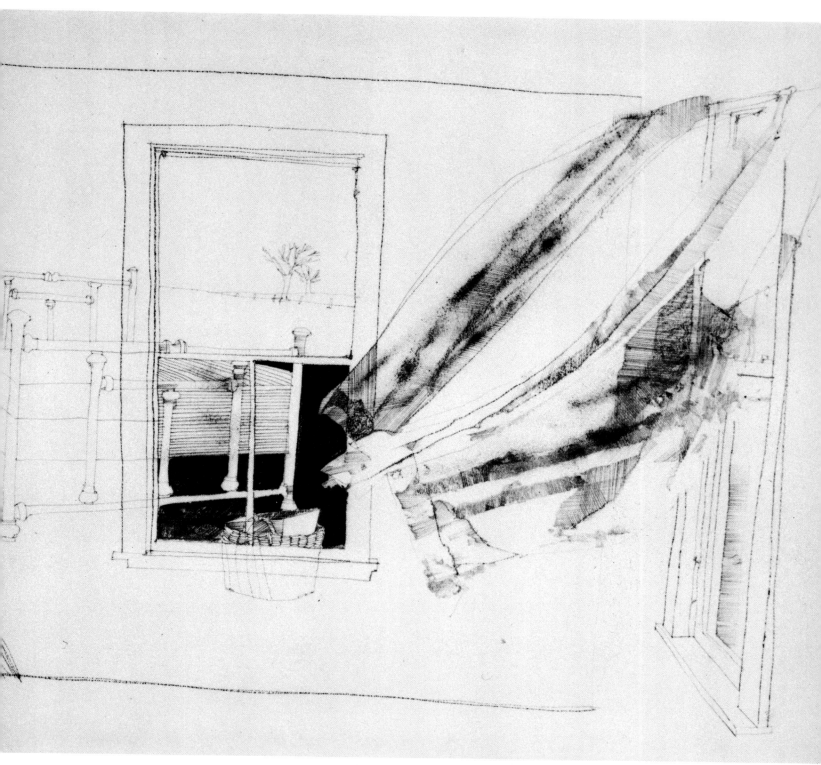

**10**
*Book*
Artist: **Robert Heindel**
Art Director: Gordon Fisher
Title: The Grapes of Wrath
Publisher: The Franklin Library

**11**
*Advertising*
Artist: **Nicholas Gaetano**
Art Director: Nicholas Gaetano
Client: Larry Gagosian/Prints
on Broxton

**12**
*Institutional*
Artist: **Murray Tinkelman**
Client: National Parks Service

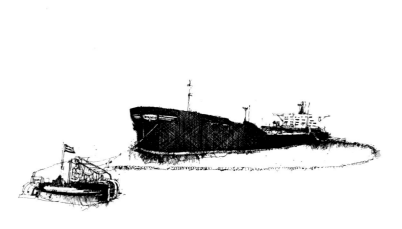

**13**
*Advertising*
Artist: **Kenneth F. Dewey**
Art Director: Ed Cencora
Agency: Benton & Bowles, Inc.
Client: Texaco

**14**
*Advertising*
Artist: **Jim Deigan**
Art Director: Joseph Kravec
Agency: Ketchum, MacLeod & Grove
Client: PPG Industries

**15**
*Advertising*
Artist: **John Berkey**
Art Director: Fred Grumm
Agency: Grey Advertising Inc.
Client: Navy Recruiting Command

BROO

CHEL

THEATRE

**16**
*Institutional*
Artist: **Doug Johnson**
Art Director: Doug Johnson/Michael David
Agency: Performing Dogs
Client: Chelsea Theatre of Brooklyn
**Award for Excellence**

**17**
*Editorial*
Artist: **Carlos Antonio Llerena**
Art Director: Richard Erlanger
Publication: Harpers Weekly

**18**
*Editorial*
Artist: **Geoffrey Moss**
Art Director: Geoffrey Moss/Stan Hinden
Publication: The Boston Globe

**19**
*Editorial*
Artist: **Brad Holland**
Art Director: Steve Heller
Publication: The New York Times

**20**
*Book*
Artist: **Ed Lindlof**
Art Director: George Lenox
Title: John Dewey: Early Works
Publisher: Southern Illinois University Press

**21**
*Editorial*
Artist: **Judith Jampel**
Art Director: Steve Heller
Publication: The New York Times

**22**
*Institutional*
Artist: **George Guzzi**
Art Director: George Guzzi/Nicholas Loscocco
Agency: Aristocrat, Inc.
Client: Aristocrat Printing Inc.

**23**
*Book*
Artist: **David McPhail**
Art Director: Robert Lowe
Title: The Bear's Bicycle
Publisher: Little, Brown & Co.

**24**
*Book*
Artist: **Marsha Winborn**
Art Director: Orval Browning
Title: Pink Pigs
Publisher: Imperial International Learning Corp.

**25**
*Institutional*
Artist: **Holly Hobbie**
Art Director: Ray Kowalski
Client: American Greetings Corp.

**26**
*Book*
Artist: **Robert LoGrippo**
Art Director: Lidia Ferrara
Title: Glory Of The Empire
Publisher: Random House, Inc.

**27**
*Book*
Artist: **Jim Conahan**
Art Director: Richard Zinn
Title: Dinosaur
Publisher: Childcraft

**28**
*Institutional*
Artist: **Don Weller**
Art Director: Don Weller
Agency: The Weller Institute
Client: Picante Press

**29**
*Editorial*
Artist: **Doug Johnson**
Art Director: Irene Ramp
Publication: Time Magazine

**30**
*Editorial*
Artist: **Bill Chambers**
Art Director: Bill Chambers

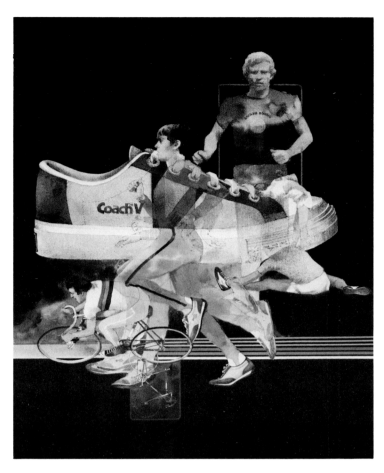

**31**
*Advertising*
Artist: **Mark Bellerose**
Art Director: Robert Cipriani/Linda Behar
Agency: Gunn Associates
Client: Converse Rubber Co.

**32**
*Institutional*
Artist: **George S. Gaadt**
Art Director: George S. Gaadt

**33**
*Book*
Artist: **Michael Nakai**
Art Director: Zlata Paces
Title: Henry Aaron & Babe Ruth Home Run Champ
Publisher: Macmillan Publishing Co.

**34**
*Advertising*
Artist: **Sandra M. Templeton**
Art Director: Sandra M. Templeton

**35**
*Editorial*
Artist: **Richard Willson**
Art Director: K. Francis Tanabe
Publication: The Washington Post

**36**
*Editorial*
Artist: **Gary Viskupic**
Art Director: Paul Back
Publication: Newsday

**37**
*Television*
Artist: **Charles McVicker**
Art Director: Charles McVicker

**38**
*Editorial*
Artist: **Vint Lawrence**
Art Director: K. Francis Tanabe
Publication: The Washington Post

**39**
*Editorial*
Artist: **Judith Jampel**
Art Director: Steve Phillips
Publication: New Times

**40**
*Advertising*
Artist: **Carlos Ochagavia**
Art Director: Jim Adair
Agency: Geer DuBois
Client: IBM

**41**
*Advertising*
Artist: **Carlos Ochagavia**
Art Director: Bob Nowak
Agency: Zakin & Comerford
Client: Broadcast Music, Inc.

**42**
*Advertising*
Artist: **Elissa Della-Piana**
Art Director: Larry Long
Agency: Gregory Fossella Assoc.
Client: Shawmut Banks

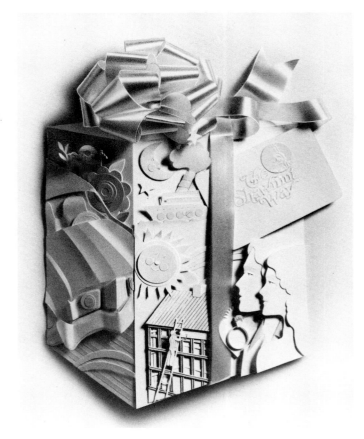

**43**
*Book*
Artist: **Judith Jampel**
Art Director: Ian Summers
Title: The Sentinel
Publisher: Ballantine Books, Inc.

**44**
*Book*
Artist: **John Sovjani**
Art Director: E.A. Burke
Title: Mind and Emotion
Publisher: John Wiley & Sons

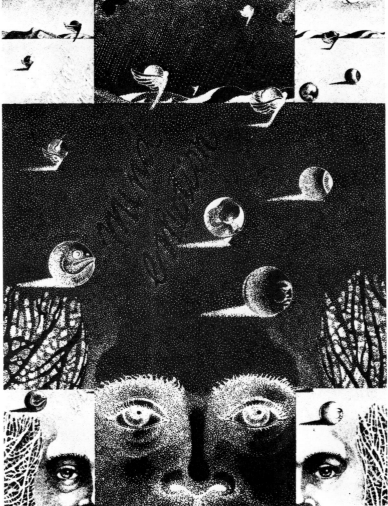

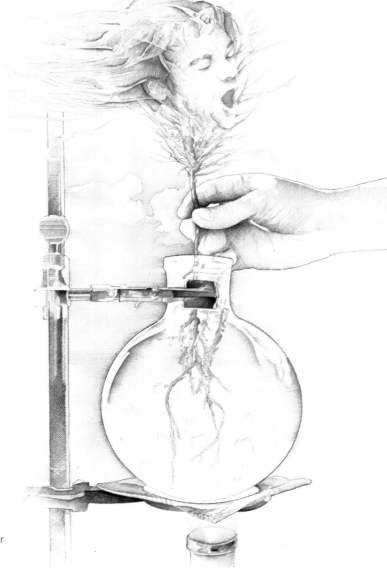

**45**
*Book*
Artist: **Paul Giovanopoulos**
Art Director: Soren Noring/Irwin Glusker
Title: The Secret Life Of Plants
Publisher: The Reader's Digest

**46**
*Book*
Artist: **Paul Giovanopoulos**
Art Director: Soren Noring/Irwin Glusker
Title: The Secret Life Of Plants
Publisher: The Reader's Digest

**47**
*Editorial*
Artist: **Mark English**
Art Director: Joe Fazio
Publication: Geigy Pharmaceuticals

**48**
*Television*
Artist/Producer: **Tom Yohe**
Animation Director: Phil Kimmelman
Production Co.: Phil Kimmelman & Associates
Client: ABC Television Network .

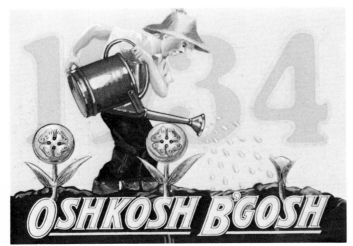

**49**
*Advertising*
Artist: **Marc Gobé**
Art Director: Marc Gobé
Client: Sonoma Vineyards

**50**
*Television*
Artist: **Spunbuggy Works, Inc.**
Art Director: David Ford Innes
Agency: Schöen-Rogers, Inc.
Client: Oshkosh B'gosh, Inc.
**Award For Excellence**

**51**
*Institutional*
Artist: **Roger Huyssen**
Art Director: John Solie
Client: CBS Television

**52**
*Advertising*
Artist: **Kim Whitesides**
Art Director: Ed Harridsloff
Agency: Diener Hauser Greenthal Co., Inc.
Client: Paramount

**53**
*Advertising*
Artist: **Shusei Nagaoka**
Art Director: Ron Wolin
Agency: Grey Advertising, Inc.
Client: American Honda Motor Inc.
**Award for Excellence**

**54**
*Television*
Artist: **Steve Karchin**
Art Director: Murlin Marsh
Client: NBC Television Network

**55**
*Television*
Artist: **Bill Greer**
Art Director: Dolores Gudzin
Client: NBC Television Network

**56**
*Advertising*
Artist: **David Palladini**
Art Director: Skip Sorvino
Client: Scholastic Magazine

**57**
*Institutional*
Artist: **Terry Steadham**
Art Director: Will Wroth
Client: Sunrise Publications, Inc.

**58**
*Television*
Artist: **Carole Jean**
Art Director: Betty Hamilton
Client: Tournament of Roses/NBC-TV

**59**
*Advertising*
Artist: **Dennis Ziemienski**
Art Director: Kirk Hinshaw
Agency: Foote, Cone & Belding, Inc.
Client: San Francisco Zoo

**60**
*Television*
Artist: **Dennis Ziemienski**
Art Director: Linda Standley
Client: Hewlett-Packard

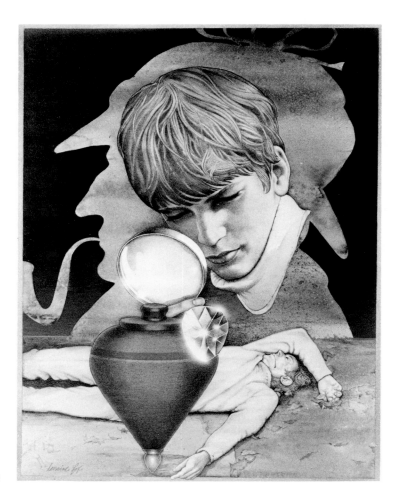

61
*Editorial*
Artist: **Lorraine Fox**
Art Director: Joe Csatari
Publication: Boys' Life Magazine

62
*Editorial*
Artist: **Mark English**
Art Director: Herb Bleiweiss
Publication: Ladies' Home Journal

**63**
*Editorial*
Artist: **Renée Faure**
Art Director: Al Conner/Max Huig
Publication: Jacksonville Magazine

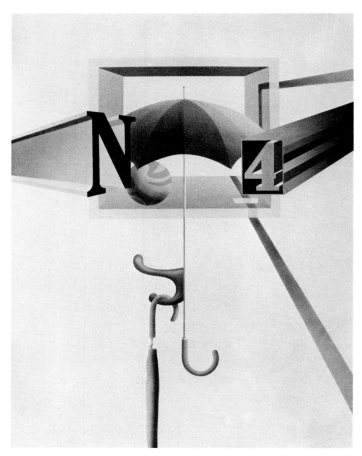

**64**
*Institutional*
Artist: **Dennis Luczak**
Art Director: Abby Spiegelman
Agency: Milea Sinclair

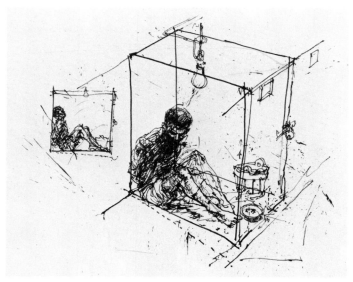

**65**
*Book*
Artist: **William Hofmann**
Art Director: Soren Noring/Irwin Glusker
Title: Prisoner Of Mao
Publisher: The Reader's Digest

**66**
*Television*
Artist: **John Sovjani**
Art Director: Murlin Marsh
Client: NBC Television Network

# THE TOP OF THE WORLD

*fiction*
By TOM MAYER

*man meets eagle in the cold arena of the sky*

**67**
*Editorial*
Artist: **Alex Ebel**
Art Director: Arthur Paul/Kerig Pope
Publication: Playboy Magazine

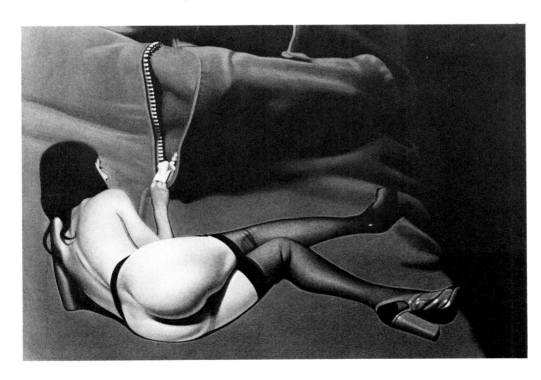

**68**
*Editorial*
Artist: **Alex Gnidziejko**
Art Director: Don Menell
Publication: Oui Magazine

**69**
*Editorial*
Artist: **Gary Cooley**
Art Director: Robert M. Dougherty
Publication: Money Magazine

**70**
*Book*
Artist: **Barbara Bergman**
Art Director: Barbara Bertoli
Title: The Victim
Publisher: Avon Books

**71**
*Book*
Artist: **Peter Lloyd**
Art Director: Barbara Bertoli
Title: Experiment At Proto
Publisher: Avon Books

**72**
*Institutional*
Artist: **Alan Magee**
Art Director: Alan Magee

**73**
*Institutional*
Artist: **Randall McKissick**
Art Director: Randall McKissick
Agency: McKissick/Illustrator
Client: Graftech Corp.

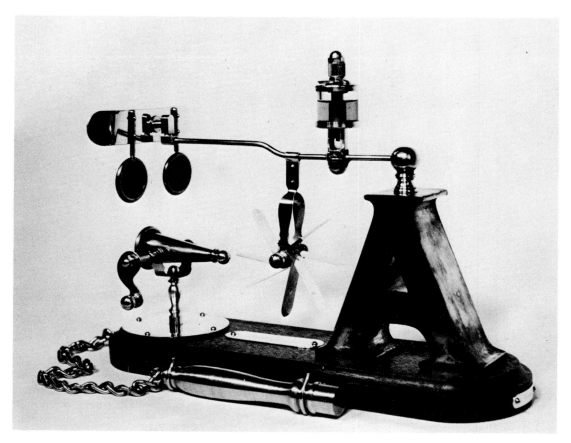

**74**
*Institutional*
Artist: **Walter Einsel**
Art Director: Walter Einsel
Client: Dr. Arnold von Feldman

**75**
*Book*
Artist: **Alan Magee**
Art Director: Milton Charles
Title: The Natural
Publisher: Pocket Books

**76**
*Book*
Artist: **Mavis Smith**
Art Director: Gerry Contreras

**77**
*Editorial*
Artist: **Gene Szafran**
Art Director: Joe Brooks
Publication: Penthouse Magazine

**78**
*Editorial*
Artist: **Charley Brown**
Art Director: Thomas Gould
Publication: Psychology Today

79
*Book*
Artist: **Marilyn Bass/Marvin Goldman**
Art Director: Marilyn Bass/Marvin Goldman
Publisher: Macmillan Publishing Co., Inc.

**80**
*Book*
Artist: **Howard Koslow**
Art Director: Milton Charles
Title: The Pocket Book of America
Publisher: Pocket Books

**81**
*Advertising*
Artist: **Chet Jezierski**
Art Director: Stan Sweeney
Agency: W.B. Doner & Co.
Client: National Guard

**82**
*Editorial*
Artist: **Gary Kelley**
Art Director: Gary Kelley

**83**
*Editorial*
Artist: **Gary Kelley**
Art Director: Gary Kelley

**84**
*Editorial*
Artist: **Richard Harvey**
Art Director: Jean-Pierre Holley
Publication: Oui Magazine

**85**
*Institutional*
Artist: **C. Royd Crosthwaite**
Art Director: C. Royd Crosthwaite

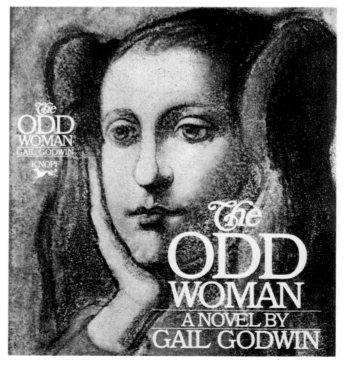

**86**
*Book*
Artist: **Daniel Maffia**
Art Director: Lidia Ferrara/Bob Scudellari
Title: The Odd Woman
Publisher: Alfred A. Knopf

**87**
*Editorial*
Artist: **Charles B. Slackman**
Art Director: Arthur Paul/Kerig Pope
Publication: Playboy Magazine

**88**
*Editorial*
Artist: **Dean Thompson**
Art Director: Dean Thompson

**89**
*Advertising*
Artist: **Leo & Diane Dillon**
Art Director: Robert Gavin
Client: Caedmon Records

90
*Institutional*
Artist: **Mark Bellerose**
Art Director: Mark Bellerose

91
*Editorial*
Artist: **Robert Grossman**
Art Director: Richard Gangel
Publication: Sports Illustrated

**92**
*Institutional*
Artist: **Peter M. Fiore**
Art Director: Gerry Contreras
Client: Pratt Institute

**93**
*Editorial*
Artist: **Sandy Huffaker**
Art Director: Eric Seidman
Publication: The New York Times

**94**
*Institutional*
Artist: **Volker Soesenbeth**
Art Director: Anders Pihlstroem
Agency: Schoenkopf & Westrell AB
Client: Svenska Pappershandlareföreningen

**95**
*Institutional*
Artist: **Volker Soesenbeth**
Art Director: Anders Pihlstroem
Agency: Schoenkopf & Westrell AB
Client: Svenska Pappershandlareföreningen

**96**
*Editorial*
Artist: **Susan Vaeth**
Art Director: Gene Krackehl
Publication: Scholastic Magazines

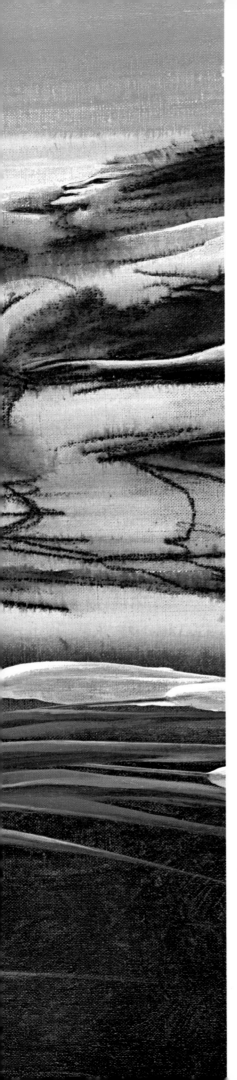

**97**
*Institutional*
Artist: **Ted Rand**
Art Director: Richard Piper
Client: United Graphics

This is one of those drawings that come to life
I love it as I love the old men in it. It is
her. It is when I draw that knowone draws
better.

97 come here from Italy (Sicily) 1894 married in 1904
arrivi duci Roma. I can sing better them
arthur Godfrey. I use to sing years ago
Did you ever hear O So lo mio. you never
hear the whole song.
8 Feb 1973

Mrs Schening

Miss Gatz

For a half an hour I drew mrs Schening getting the impression she didn't know I was there let alone drawing. Someone walked by and asked her "why she didn't smile for the man" she said that "If he told me who he was and that he wanted me to smile I would have smiled". "I fainted"

Alan E. Cober
2 June 1972
Westedge Nursing.

**99**
*Book*
Artist: **Alan E. Cober**
Art Director: Sam Antupit/Paul Kennedy
Title: The Forgotten Society
Publisher: Dover Publishing Co.
**Gold Medal**

**98**
*Book*
Artist: **Alan E. Cober**
Art Director: Sam Antupit/Paul Kennedy
Title: The Forgotten Society
Publisher: Dover Publishing Co.

**100**
*Institutional*
Artist: **Allen M. Welkis**
Art Director: Ira Silberlicht
Client: Emergency Medicine

**101**
*Editorial*
Artist: **Alex Gnidziejko**
Art Director: Don Menell
Publication: Oui Magazine
**Gold Medal**

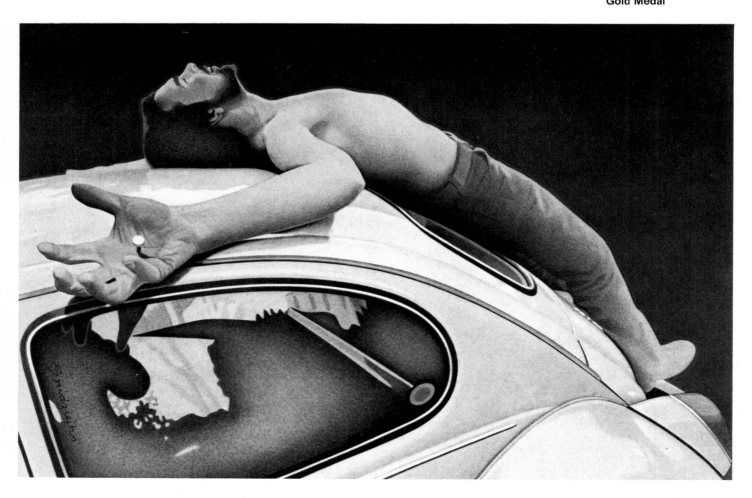

**102**
*Television*
Artist: **John Sovjani**
Art Director: Murlin Marsh
Client: NBC Television Network

**103**
*Editorial*
Artist: **Roger Huyssen**
Art Director: Peter Rauch/Robert M. Dougherty
Publication: Money Magazine

**104**
*Editorial*
Artist: **Oni**
Art Director: John Bradford
Publication: Family Circle

**105**
*Book*
Artist: **Carol Inouye**
Art Director: Marion Davis
Title: Frontispiece, Winter 1975
Publisher: The Reader's Digest

**106**
*Book*
Artist: **Tien Ho**
Art Director: Tien Ho

**107**
*Book*
Artist: **Tien Ho**
Art Director: Tien Ho

**108**
*Book*
Artist: **Tien Ho**
Art Director: Tien Ho

**109**
*Editorial*
Artist: **Dennis Luczak**
Art Director: Joe Brooks
Publication: Penthouse Magazine

**110**
*Editorial*
Artist: **Don Weller**
Art Director: Robert Carpenter
Publication: Playgirl Magazine

**111**
*Book*
Artist: **Faith M. Towle**
Art Director: Walter Lorraine
Title: The Magic Cooking Pot
Publisher: Houghton Mifflin Co.

**112**
*Institutional*
Artist: **AB Nordbok**
Art Director: Harry O. Diamond
Client: Exxon Corporation

**113**
*Book*
Artist: **Robert E. McGinnis**
Art Director: Barbara Bertoli
Title: Run
Publisher: Avon Books

**114**
*Book*
Artist: **George Ziel**
Art Director: Ian Summers/Lee Fishbach
Title: The Witches are Back
Publisher: Ballantine Books, Inc.

**115**
*Book*
Artist: **Howard Terpning**
Art Director: Marion Davis
Title: Lost!
Publisher: The Reader's Digest

**116**
*Advertising*
Artist: **Carl Chaplin**
Art Director: Graham Hallek/Jerry Green
Agency: McKim Advertising
Client: CKNW Broadcasting

**117**
*Institutional*
Artist: **Philip Smith**
Art Director: Philip Smith

**118**
*Institutional*
Artist: **Braulio Calaustro, Jr.**
Art Director: Braulio Calaustro, Jr.
Client: Delli, Carpini, Kaylor, Inc.

119
*Book*
Artist: **Leonard Baskin**
Art Director: Kathleen Westray
Title: Season Songs
Publisher: The Viking Press

120
*Advertising*
Artist: **Milton Glaser**
Art Director: Paula Scher
Client: Atlantic Records

**121**
*Advertising*
Artist: **Gervasio Gallardo**
Art Director: Joe Fazio
Agency: Geigy Pharmaceuticals
Client: Geigy in House
**Gold Medal**

**122**
*Editorial*
Artist: **Donald Moss**
Art Director: Richard Gangel
Publication: Sports Illustrated

**123**
Artist: **Wilson McLean**
Art Director: Alan Goodman
Agency: Leber, Katz Partners
Client: Utica National Insurance Group

**124**
*Institutional*
Artist: **Bob Peak**
Art Director: Don Smolen
Agency: Smolen, Smith & Connolly
Client: United Artists

**125**
*Institutional*
Artist: **Lew McCance**
Art Director: Irwin Glusker
Client: Mobil Oil Corp.

126
*Book*
Artist: **John Groth**
Art Director: William Wittliff
Title: The Last Running
Publisher: Encino Press

127
*Editorial*
Artist: **Daniel Schwartz**
Art Director: Richard Gangel
Publication: Sports Illustrated

**128**
*Institutional*
Artist: **Barron Storey**
Art Director: Elmer Yochum
Agency: Ketchum, MacLeod & Grove
Client: Scott Paper Company

**129**
*Book*
Artist: **Wendell Minor**
Art Director: Carolyn Anthony
Title: The Twilight Seas
Publisher: Weybright & Talley

**131**
*Advertising*
Artist: **Ed Sorel**
Art Director: John Berg/Henrietta Condak
Client: CBS Records

**130**
*Book*
Artist: **Robert S. Lowery**
Art Director: Robert S. Lowery

**132**
*Book*
Artist: **Thomas Upshur**
Art Director: James Plumeri
Title: Billion Dollar Baby
Publisher: New American Library

**133**
*Advertising*
Artist: **Ray Domingo**
Art Director: Jim Hedden
Agency: Bill Gold Advertising, Inc.
Client: Warner Brothers, Inc.

**134**
*Editorial*
Artist: **Ronald D. Kriss**
Art Director: Thomas Gould
Publication: Psychology Today

**135**
*Editorial*
Artist: **Jözef Sumichrast**
Art Director: Jözef Sumichrast

**136**
*Advertising*
Artist: **Clifford Condak**
Art Director: John Berg/Henrietta Condak
Client: CBS Records

**137**
*Book*
Artist: **Betty Fraser**
Art Director: Zlata Paces
Title: The Secret Of The Gourmandy (Solo Book Series R)
Publisher: Macmillan Publishing Co.

**138**
*Advertising*
Artist: **Daniel Maffia**
Art Director: Paula Scher
Client: Atlantic Records

**139**
*Editorial*
Artist: **Dickran Palulian**
Art Director: Joe Brooks
Publication: Penthouse

**140**
*Editorial*
Artist: **Don Ivan Punchatz**
Art Director: Jean-Pierre Holley
Publication: Oui Magazine

**141**
*Editorial*
Artist: **David Palladini**
Art Director: Leo F. McCarthy
Publication: Swank Magazine

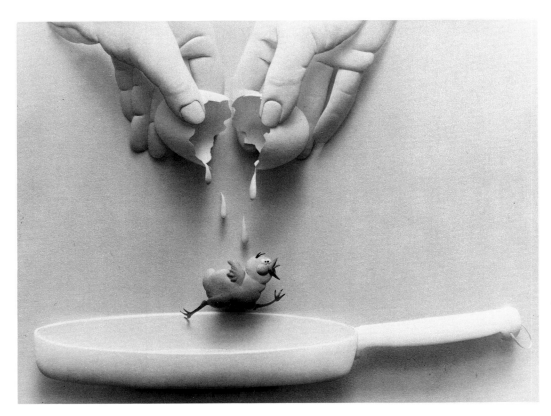

**142**
*Institutional*
Artist: **Siegbert Reinhard**
Art Director: Siegbert Reinhard
Client: Ira Roberts Publishing Co.

**143**
*Advertising*
Artist: **Siegbert Reinhard**
Art Director: Siegbert Reinhard
Client: Gerald & Cullen Rapp

**144**
*Institutional*
Artist: **Siegbert Reinhard**
Art Director: Siegbert Reinhard
Client: Ira Roberts Publishing Co.

**145**
*Institutional*
Artist: **Siegbert Reinhard**
Art Director: Siegbert Reinhard
Client: Gerald & Cullen Rapp

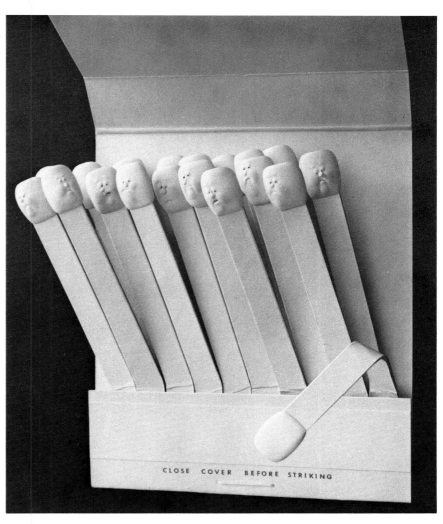

CLOSE COVER BEFORE STRIKING

**150**
*Editorial*
Artist: **Anthony Saris**
Art Director: Joe Csatari
Publication: Boys' Life Magazine

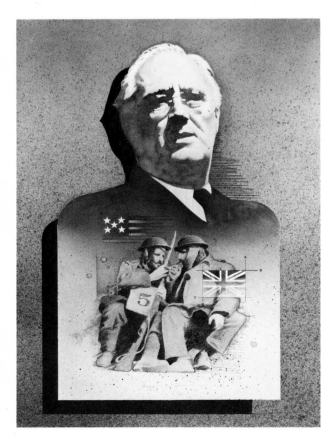

**151**
*Institutional*
Artist: **Reagan Wilson**
Art Director: Reagan Wilson

**152**
*Advertising*
Artist: **Gene Wilkes**
Art Director: Chuck Kelley
Agency: Chuck Kelley Design
Client: Male Slacks

**153**
*Institutional*
Artist: **Dick Kohfield**
Art Director: Dick Kohfield
Client: U.S. Air Force

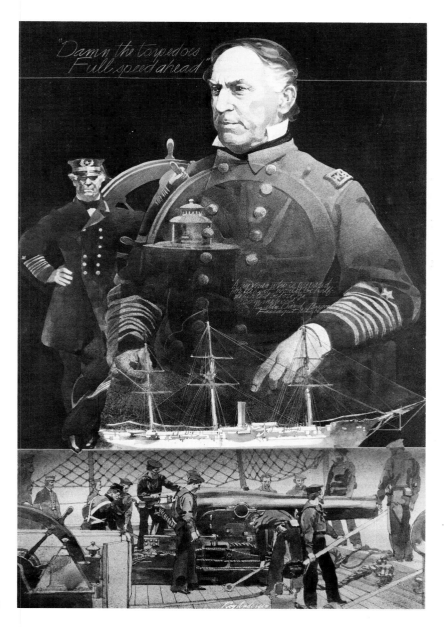

**154**
*Book*
Artist: **Roy H. Andersen**
Art Director: Roy H. Andersen

155
*Editorial*
Artist: **Mort Drucker**
Art Director: David Merrill
Publication: Time Magazine

MID-EAST
IS PEACE
AT HAND?

**156**
*Editorial*
Artist: **David Levine**
Art Director: Michael Brent
Publication: Institutional Investor Magazine

**157**
*Book*
Artist: **David Levine**
Art Director: Lidia Ferrara
Title: A World Destroyed
Publisher: Alfred A. Knopf

**158**
*Editorial*
Artist: **Brad Holland**
Art Director: Arthur Paul/Bob Post
Publication: Playboy Magazine

**159**
*Book*
Artist: **Ed Soyka**
Art Director: Milton Charles
Title: The Best Of John Collier
Publisher: Pocket Books

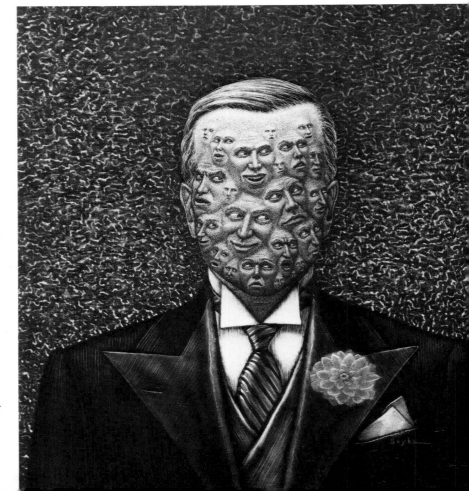

160
*Advertising*
Artist: **David Wilcox**
Art Director: Paula Scher
Client: Atlantic Records

161
*Editorial*
Artist: **David Schleinkofer**
Art Director: Borys Patchowsky
Publication: Stereo Review

**162**
*Editorial*
Artist: **Geoffrey Moss**
Art Director: Geoffrey Moss
Publication: The Boston Globe

**163**
*Book*
Artist: **Brad Holland**
Art Director: Frances McCullough
Title: The Geek
Publisher: Harper & Row Publishers, Inc.

**164**
*Advertising*
Artist: **Philip Garris**
Art Director: Bob Cato
Agency: United Artist Records
Client: Grateful Dead Records
**Gold Medal**

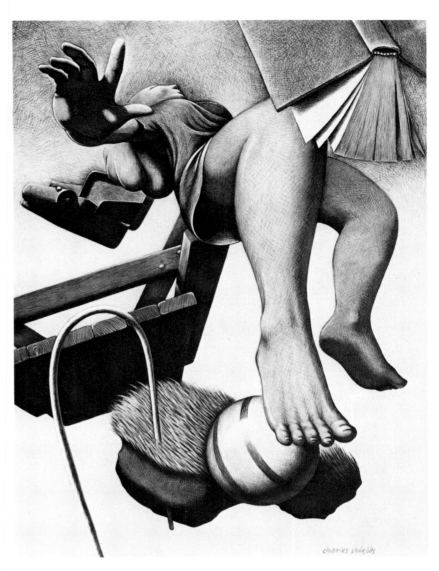

**165**
*Editorial*
Artist: **Charles Shields**
Art Director: Charles Shields

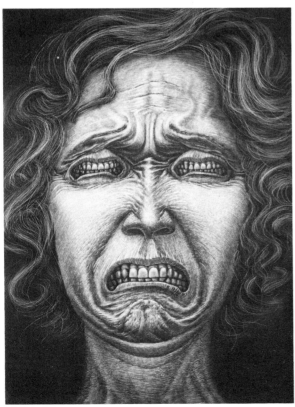

**166**
*Editorial*
Artist: **Ed Soyka**
Art Director: Ira Silberlicht/Tom Lennon
Publication: Emergency Medicine

**167**
*Advertising*
Artist: **Jerry Pinkney**
Art Director: Ralph Moxcey
Agency: Humphrey, Browning, MacDougall
Client: Warren Paper

168
*Book*
Artist: **Jerry Pinkney**
Art Director: Peter Landa
Title: Mouse & Cat
Publisher: Frederick Warne Co.

**169**
*Advertising*
Artist: **Judy Clifford**
Art Director: Steven Jacobs
Agency: Steven Jacobs Design
Client: Simpson Lee Paper Co.

**170**
*Editorial*
Artist: **Bernard Fuchs**
Art Director: Ken Jordan/John DeCesare
Publication: Geigy Pharmaceuticals

**171**
*Book*
Artist: **Fred Otnes**
Art Director: Charles O. Hyman
Title: "We Americans"
Publisher: National Geographic Society
**Award For Excellence**

**172**
*Advertising*
Artist: **Fred Otnes**
Art Director: Vince Maiello
Agency: Doubleday & Co.
Client: The Literary Guild

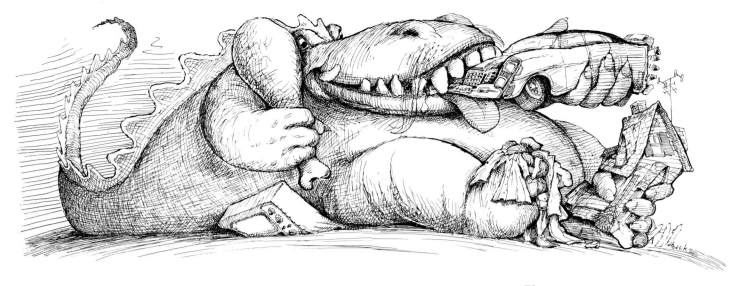

**173**
*Editorial*
Artist: **Stan Mack**
Art Director: Samuel N. Antupit
Publication: J.C. Penney Forum

Something for Everybody from U&lc.

ILLUSTRATED BY MURRAY TINKELMAN

**EIGHT WAYS TO ACHIEVE THE HEIGHTS AND/OR DEPTHS TO WHICH MEN ASPIRE**

**(1)**
I have found some of the best reasons I ever had for remaining at the bottom simply by looking at the men at the top.
FRANK COLBY

**(2)**
Women have served all these centuries as looking glasses possessing the magic and delicious power of reflecting the figure of a man at twice his natural size.
VIRGINIA WOOLF

**(3)**
Sits he on so high a throne, a man still sits on his bottom.
MONTAIGNE

**(4)**
Heights were made to be looked at, not looked from.
GILBERT CHESTERTON

**(5)**
Happiness makes up in height what it lacks in length.
ROBERT FROST

**(6)**
Better put a strong fence 'round the top of a cliff than an ambulance down in the valley.
JOSEPH MALINES

**(7)**
If you would go up high, then use your own legs! Do not get yourselves carried aloft; do not seat yourselves on other people's backs and heads.
NIETZSCHE

**(8)**
Only when man is safely ensconced under six feet of earth, with several tons of granite upon his chest, is he in a position to give advice with any certainty and then he is silent.
A. EDWARD NEWTON

THIS ARTICLE WAS SET IN SOUVENIR ITALIC

**174**
*Editorial*
Artist: **Murray Tinkelman**
Art Director: Herb Lubalin
Client: U&lc

**175**
*Advertising*
Artist: **Maurice Lewis**
Art Director: Harold Hutcheson
Agency: Ogilvy & Mather Inc.
Client: Shell Oil Co.

**176**
*Book*
Artist: **Michael Kelly Williams**
Art Director: Brenda Patterson

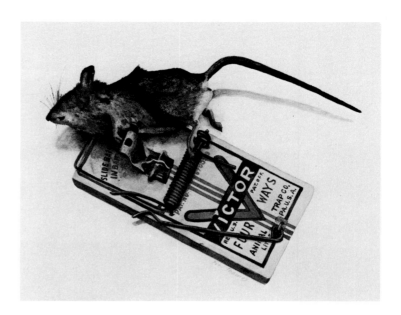

**177**
*Advertising*
Artist: **Fred W. Thomas**
Art Director: Fred W. Thomas

**178**
*Book*
Artist: **Robert Shore**
Art Director: Robert Shore
Title: Confidence Man
Publisher: Ronile Press

**179**
*Television*
Artist: **Robert Heindel**
Art Director: Jack Bratman
Client: Exxon Corporation

**180**
*Editorial*
Artist: **Robert E. Lapsley**
Art Director: Robert E. Lapsley

181
*Institutional*
Artist: **Robert M. Cunningham**
Art Director: Elaine Rooney
Agency: Chermayeff & Geismar Assocs.
Client: American Revolution Bicentennial

**182**
*Advertising*
Artist: **Gralyn Holmstrom**
Art Director: Gralyn Holmstrom
Client: Jane Lander Associates

183
*Editorial*
Artist: **Wilson McLean**
Art Director: Linda Cox
Publication: Cosmopolitan Magazine

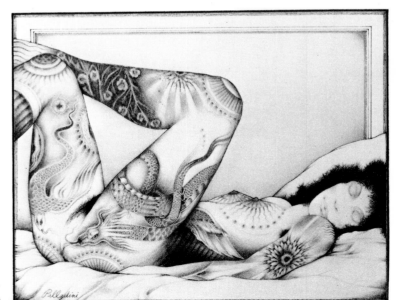

184
*Editorial*
Artist: **David Palladini**
Art Director: Leo F. McCarthy
Publication: Swank Magazine

185
*Advertising*
Artist: **Dick Harvey**
Art Director: Joseph Stelmach
Client: RCA Records

186
*Advertising*
Artist: **John M. Thompson**
Art Director: John M. Thompson
Client: Cappac Farms

**187**
*Advertising*
Artist: **John M. Thompson**
Art Director: Dave Falcon
Agency: Tromson, Monroe
Client: Curacao Tourist Board

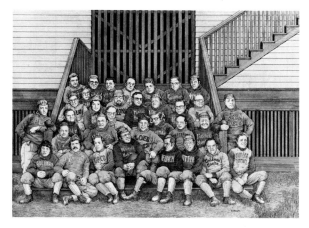

**188**
*Editorial*
Artist: **Robert VanNutt**
Art Director: Michael Brent
Publication: Institutional Investor

**189**
*Book*
Artist: **Robert Heindel**
Art Director: Soren Noring/Irwin Glusker
Title: Sybil
Publisher: The Reader's Digest
**Award for Excellence**

**190**
*Advertising*
Artist: **Dan Long**
Art Director: Dan Long

**191**
*Book*
Artist: **Wendell Minor**
Art Director: Char Lappan
Title: Architecture Of The Arkansas Ozarks
Publisher: Little, Brown & Co.

192
*Institutional*
Artist: **Robert Andrew Parker**
Art Director: Harry O. Diamond
Client: Exxon Corporation
**Award for Excellence**

193
*Advertising*
Artist: **Robert Andrew Parker**
Art Director: John Berg
Client: CBS Records

194
*Book*
Artist: **The Quays (Steve & Tim)**
Art Director: Betty Anderson
Title: The Clockwork Testament
Publisher: Alfred A. Knopf

195
*Institutional*
Artist: **Richard Hess**
Art Director: Richard Hess
Client: Franklin Typographers

**196**
*Advertising*
Artist: **Bob Peak**
Art Director: Don Smolen
Agency: Smolen, Smith & Connolly
Client: United Artists

**197**
*Editorial*
Artist: **Barron Storey**
Art Director: Leo F. McCarthy
Publication: Swank Magazine

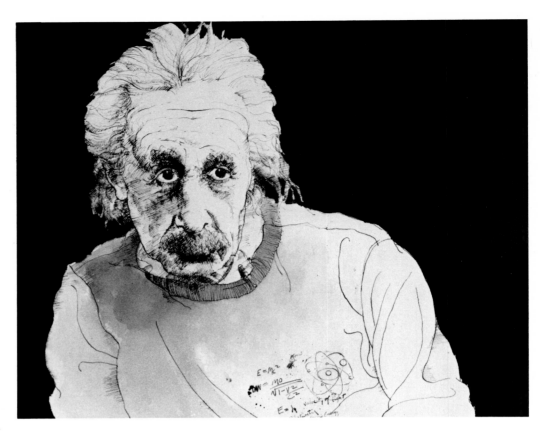

**198**
*Editorial*
Artist: **Joe Ciardiello**
Art Director: Joe Ciardiello

**199**
*Institutional*
Artist: **Joe Ciardiello**
Art Director: Joe Ciardiello

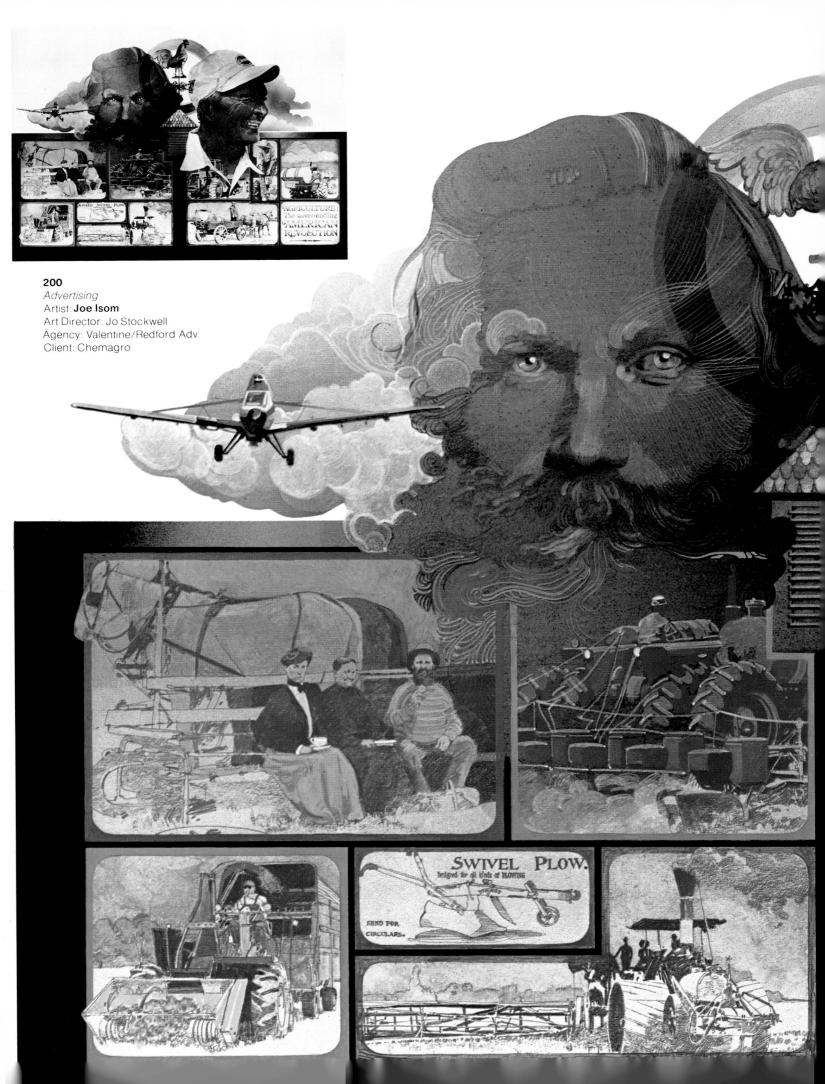

**200**
*Advertising*
Artist: **Joe Isom**
Art Director: Jo Stockwell
Agency: Valentine/Redford Adv.
Client: Chemagro

201
*Editorial*
Artist: **Dick Harvey**
Art Director: Jessica M. Weber/Salvatore Lazzarotti
Publication: Guideposts Magazine

202
*Editorial*
Artist: **Franklin McMahon**
Art Director: Richard Gangel
Publication: Sports Illustrated

**203**
*Institutional*
Artist: **Erik Sundgaard**
Art Director: Erik Sundgaard

**204**
*Institutional*
Artist: **Erik Sundgaard**
Art Director: Erik Sundgaard

**205**
*Book*
Artist: **Victor G. Ambrus**
Art Director: Will Winslow
Title: A Country Wedding
Publisher: Addison-Wesley Publishing Co.

**206**
*Institutional*
Artist: **Len Berzofsky**
Art Director: Len Berzofsky
Client: ABC-TV

**207**
*Television*
Artist: **Len Berzofsky**
Art Director: Len Berzofsky
Client: WABC Eyewitness News

**208**
*Advertising*
Artist: **Roy Carruthers**
Art Director: James Ong
Agency: Ong & Associates
Client: WLS-TV

**209**
*Editorial*
Artist: **Bill Chambers**
Art Director: Bill Chambers

**210**
*Editorial*
Artist: **Bill Chambers**
Art Director: Bill Chambers

**212**
*Book*
Artist: **Gerry Gersten**
Art Director: Robert Kingsbury
Title: Pubus
Publisher: Straight Arrow Books

**213**
*Institutional*
Artist: **Haruo Miyauchi**
Art Director: Seymour Chwast
Client: Push Pin Studios

**211**
*Editorial*
Artist: **Ronald D. Kriss**
Art Director: Thomas Gould
Publication: Psychology Today

**214**
*Book*
Artist: **Robert Byrd**
Art Director: Robert Byrd

**215**
*Book*
Artist: **Denise Saldutti**
Art Director: Denise Saldutti

**216**
*Book*
Artist: **Diane Dawson**
Art Director: Diane Dawson

**217**
*Book*
Artist: **Richard Egielski**
Art Director: Richard Egielski

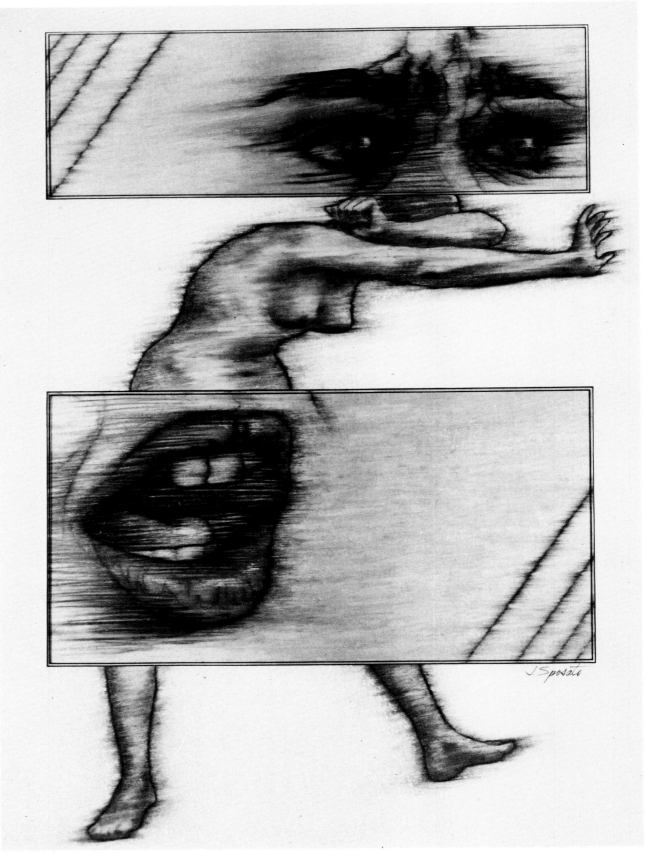

**218**
*Book*
Artist: **John Sposato**
Art Director: Lucy Fehr
Title: Incubus
Publisher: William Morrow Co.

**219**
*Editorial*
Artist: **Teresa Fasolino**
Art Director: Bea Feitler
Publication: Ms Magazine

**220**
*Editorial*
Artist: **Jean Leon Huens**
Art Director: Howard E. Paine
Publication: National Geographic Magazine

**221**
*Editorial*
Artist: **Jean Leon Huens**
Art Director: Howard E. Paine
Publication: National Geographic Magazine

**222**
*Book*
Artist: **Richard F. Newton**
Art Director: Robert Amft
Client: Scott, Foresman & Co.

**223**
*Advertising*
Artist: **Wilson McLean**
Art Director: Herbert Levitt
Agency: Wells, Rich & Green
Client: Benson & Hedges

**224**
*Institutional*
Artist: **David Kilmer**
Art Director: Dallas Powell

**225**
*Advertising*
Artist: **Joseph M. Ovies**
Art Director: Joseph M. Ovies

**226**
*Editorial*
Artist: **Carl Chaplin**
Art Director: Kerig Pope
Publication: Playboy Magazine

**229**
*Book*
Artist: **Herb Tauss**
Art Director: Leonard Leone
Title: Threshold
Publisher: Bantam Books

**228**
*Book*
Artist: **Daniel Schwartz**
Art Director: Soren Noring
Title: Chief
Publisher: The Reader's Digest

**230**
*Book*
Artist: **Tom Wilkes**
Art Director: Diana Klemin
Title: Lilly On Dolphins
Publisher: Doubleday & Co., Inc.

**227**
*Editorial*
Artist: **Alan E. Cober**
Art Director: Robert Hallock
Publication: Lithopinion

**231**
*Institutional*
Artist: **Charles Santore**
Art Director: Toby Schmidt
Client: Children's Hospital of Philadelphia

**232**
*Editorial*
Artist: **Rick Meyrowitz**
Art Director: Peter Kleinman
Publication: National Lampoon

**233**
*Book*
Artist: **Leo & Diane Dillon**
Art Director: Kathleen Westray/Linda Zuckerman
Title: The Hundred Penny Box
Publisher: The Viking Press

**234**
*Advertising*
Artist: **Lane Yerkes**
Art Director: Lane Yerkes

**235**
*Editorial*
Artist: **Mark English**
Art Director: Herb Bleiweiss
Publication: Ladies' Home Journal

**236**
*Advertising*
Artist: **Gervasio Gallardo**
Art Director: Elmer Pizzi
Agency: Gray & Rogers, Inc.
Client: Grit

**237**
*Advertising*
Artist: **Jean Mulatier**
Art Director: Elmer Pizzi
Agency: Gray & Rogers
Client: Grit

**238**
*Advertising*
Artist: **Ed Samuels**
Art Director: John Berg
Client: CBS Records

**239**
*Editorial*
Artist: **Alexander Gnidziejko**
Art Director: Don Menell
Publication: Oui Magazine

**240**
*Book*
Artist: **Robert Andrew Parker**
Art Director: Atha Tehon
Title: Izzie
Publisher: The Dial Press

**241**
*Book*
Artist: **Bill Goldsmith**
Art Director: Louise Noble
Title: All About Apples
Publisher: Houghton Mifflin Co.

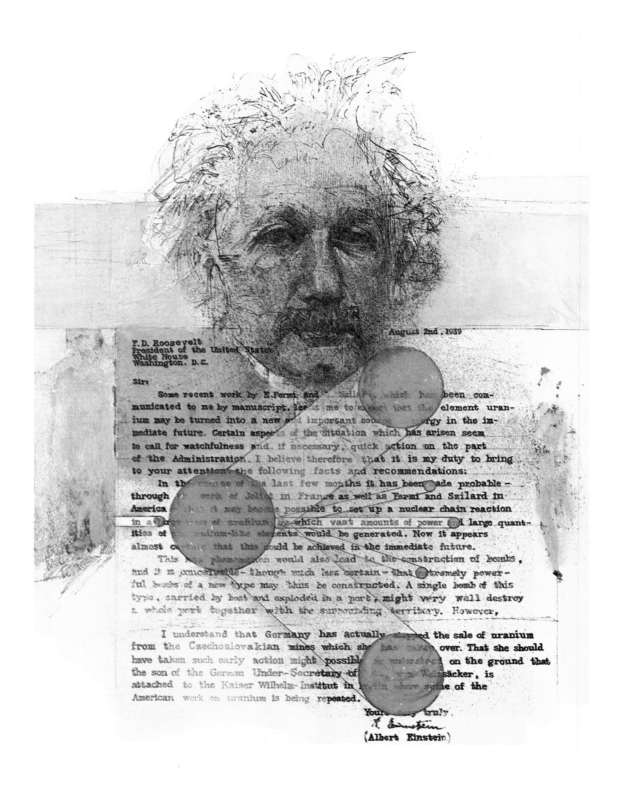

**242**
*Institutional*
Artist: **Barron Storey**
Art Director: Elmer Yochum
Agency: Ketchum, MacLeod & Grove
Client: Scott Paper Company

**243**
*Institutional*
Artist: **Barron Storey**
Art Director: Elmer Yochum
Agency: Ketchum, MacLeod & Grove
Client: Scott Paper Company

**244**
*Television*
Artist: **Judith Hoffman Corwin**
Art Director: George Pierson
Client: NBC Television Network

**245**
*Advertising*
Artist: **Bruce Wolfe**
Art Director: David Bartels
Agency: Clinton E. Frank
Client: Deans Foods Co.

**246**
*Editorial*
Artist: **Don Weller**
Art Director: David Merrill
Publication: Time Magazine

247
*Editorial*
Artist: **Joe Isom**
Art Director: Nick Brocker
Publication: Wee Wisdom

248
*Advertising*
Artist: **Joe Isom**
Art Director: Guinotte Wise
Agency: Valentine/Radford Adv.
Client: McNally-Pittsburg

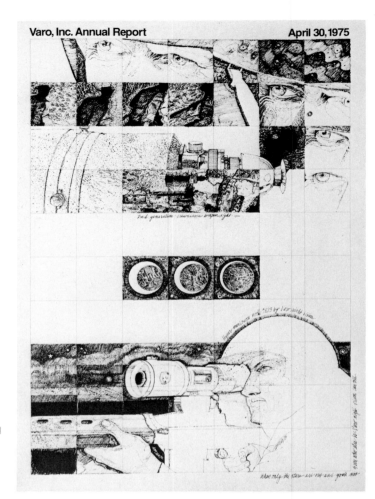

**249**
*Institutional*
Artist: **Jack Unruh**
Art Director: Jack Summerford
Agency: Richards Group
Client: Varo Inc.

**250**
*Book*
Artist: **Boris Vallejo**
Art Director: Ian Summers
Title: Of Man And Monsters
Publisher: Ballantine Books, Inc.

**251**
*Book*
Artist: **Christopher J. Spollen**
Art Director: Cathy Altholz
Title: Tales From The Steppes
Publisher: Coward. McCann & Geoghegan, Inc.

**252**
*Advertising*
Artist: **Nicholas Gaetano**
Art Director: Ken Jordan
Client: Geigy Pharmaceuticals

**253**
*Advertising*
Artist: **Clifford Condak**
Art Director: John Berg
Client: CBS Records

**254**
*Advertising*
Artist: **Ted CoConis**
Art Director: Talivaldis Stubis
Agency: Bill Gold Advertising, Inc.
Client: Warner Brothers

**255**
*Advertising*
Artist: **Ted CoConis**
Art Director: Steven Blanco
Agency: Cannon Advertising, Inc.
Client: Mexican National Tourist Council

256
*Book*
Artist: **Ted CoConis**
Art Director: Ian Summers
Title: The Princess Bride
Publisher: Ballantine Books, Inc.

257
*Editorial*
Artist: **Ted CoConis**
Art Director: Linda Cox
Publication: Cosmopolitan Magazine

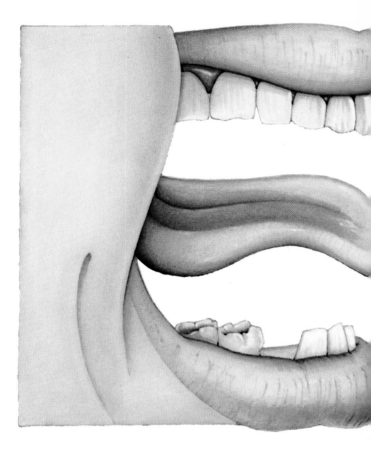

**258**
*Institutional*
Artist: **Jözef Sumichrast**
Art Director: Jözef Sumichrast
Client: Jim Berntsen & Associates

**259**
*Advertising*
Artist: **Lee Bonner**
Art Director: John Pringle
Agency: W. B. Doner & Co.
Client: Commercial Credit

**260**
*Advertising*
Artist: **Walt Spitzmiller**
Art Director: Vince Maiello
Client: Doubleday & Co. (Literary Guild)

**261**
*Book*
Artist: **Shelley Freshman**
Art Director: Linda Holiday
Title: Cricket
Publisher: Bobbs-Merrill Publishing Co.

**317**
*Advertising*
Artist: **John Berkey**
Art Director: Ed Brodkin
Agency: Diener-Hauser-Greenthal Co., Inc.
Client: 20th Century-Fox

316
*Editorial*
Artist: **Dennis Luczak**
Art Director: Rowan Johnson/
　　　　　　Claire Victor/George Moy
Publication: Viva Magazine

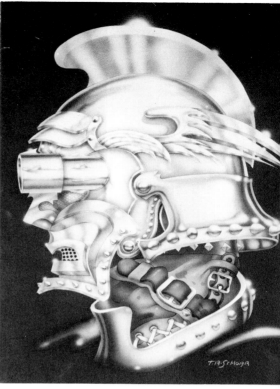

**319**
*Editorial*
Artist: **Todd Schorr**
Art Director: Todd Schorr

**320**
*Advertising*
Artist: **Jeffrey A. Schrier**
Art Director: Ed Thrasher
Client: Warner Bros. Records

318
*Book*
Artist: **Brad Holland**
Art Director: Frances McCullough
Title: The Geek
Publisher: Harper & Row Publishers, Inc.
**Gold Medal**

**310**
*Advertising*
Artist: **Harry J. Schaare**
Art Director: Harry J. Schaare

**311**
*Advertising*
Artist: **Paul Melia**
Art Director: Paul Melia

**309**
*Book*
Artist: **Max Velthuijs**
Art Director: Will Winslow
Title: The Painter and The Bird
Publisher: Addison-Wesley Publishing Co., Inc.

307
*Book*
Artist: **Nick Aristovulos**
Art Director: Linda Holiday/Gail Ash
Title: In The Wake Of Man
Publisher: Bobbs Merrill Publishing Co.

308
*Advertising*
Artist: **Richard Sparks**
Art Director: Bob Feldgus
Client: Scholastic Book Services

**304**
*Institutional*
Artist: **Lucas R. Visser**
Art Director: Lucas R. Visser
Agency: University Design
Client: Total Design

**305**
*Editorial*
Artist: **Lee Rosenblatt**
Art Director: Peter Kleinman
Publication: National Lampoon

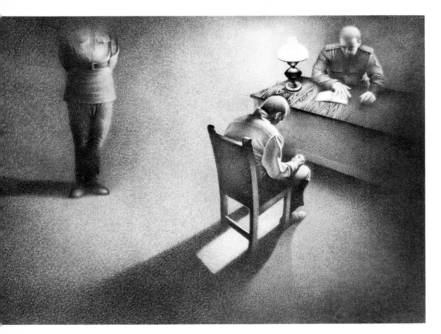

**306**
*Book*
Artist: **Jack Endewelt**
Art Director: William Gregory
Title: Alexander Dolgun's Story
Publisher: The Reader's Digest

**303**
*Institutional*
Artist: **Ted CoConis**
Art Director: Talivaldis Stubis
Agency: Bill Gold Advertising, Inc.
Client: Warner Bros. Inc.

GERALD McCONNELL
©1975

**302**
*Institutional*
Artist: **Gerald McConnell**
Art Director: Gerald McConnell
Client: National Parks Service

**300**
*Editorial*
Artist: **Paul Giovanopoulos**
Art Director: Paul Giovanopoulos

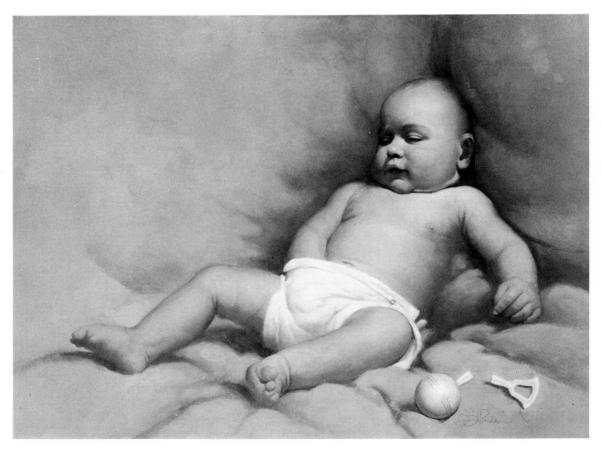

**301**
*Editorial*
Artist: **Jerry Podwil**
Art Director: Arthur Paul/Gordon Mortensen
Publication: Playboy Magazine

**298**
*Editorial*
Artist: **Daniel Schwartz**
Art Director: William Cadge
Publication: Redbook

**299**
*Advertising*
Artist: **Bob Peak**
Art Director: Talivaldis Stubis
Agency: Bill Gold Advertising, Inc.
Client: Warner Bros. Inc.

**297**
*Book*
Artist: **Fred Otnes**
Art Director: James Plumeri
Title: Europe Reborn
Publisher: New American Library

**296**
*Book*
Artist: **Fred Otnes**
Art Director: Tom Clemente/Lynne Moran
Title: 1976 Newspaper Plan Book
Publisher: Daily Newspapers of U.S.A.
        & Canada

**295**
*Book*
Artist: **Piero Ventura**
Art Director: Grace Clarke
Title: Piero Ventura's Book Of Cities
Publisher: Random House, Inc.
**Award for Excellence**

**294**
*Book*
Artist: **Piero Ventura**
Art Director: Grace Clarke
Title: Piero Ventura's Book Of Cities
Publisher: Random House, Inc.

**291**
*Editorial*
Artist: **Lionel Kalish**
Art Director: Linda Cox
Publication: Cosmopolitan Magazine

**292**
*Editorial*
Artist: **Richard Bober**
Art Director: Linda Cox
Publication: Cosmopolitan Magazine

**293**
*Advertising*
Artist: **Larry Tople**
Art Director: Art Morat
Agency: D'Arcy, MacManus & Masius
Client: Detroit Diesel Allison

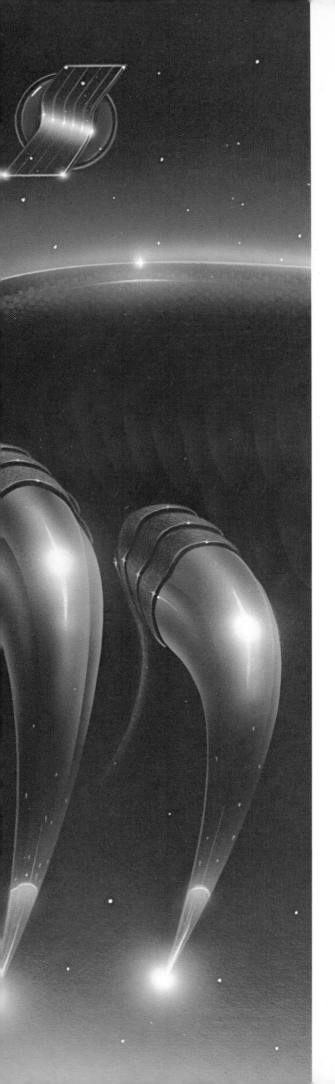

**290**
*Advertising*
Artist: **Peter Lloyd**
Art Director: Ed Lee
Client: CBS Records
**Award for Excellence**

**288**
*Book*
Artist: **Holland S. Macdonald**
Art Director: Holland S. Macdonald

**289**
*Editorial*
Artist: **Daniel Schwartz**
Art Director: Bert Sugar
Publication: Argosy

**286**
*Editorial*
Artist: **John Collier**
Art Director: William Cadge
Publication: Redbook

**287**
*Editorial*
Artist: **John Collier**
Art Director: William Cadge
Publication: Redbook

**284**
*Editorial*
Artist: **Jim Sharpe**
Art Director: David Merrill
Publication: Time Magazine

**285**
*Editorial*
Artist: **Jim Sharpe**
Art Director: David Merrill
Publication: Time Magazine

**281**
*Television*
Artist: **Jon McIntosh**
Art Director: Jon McIntosh
Client: Charles E. Merrill Co.

**282**
*Book*
Artist: **Mark Barensfeld**
Art Director: Mark Barensfeld

**283**
*Editorial*
Artist: **David Jarvis**
Art Director: Scott Reid
Publication: Forum for Contemporary
          History-Skeptic Magazine

**278**
*Advertising*
Artist: **Jim Campbell**
Art Director: Dolores Gudzin
Client: National Broadcasting Co.

**279**
*Institutional*
Artist: **Judith Jampel**
Art Director: Judith Jampel

**280**
*Editorial*
Artist: **Chris Duke**
Art Director: Chris Duke

**275**
*Television*
Artist/Producer: **Tom Yohe**
Animation Director: Phil Kimmelman
Production Co.: Phil Kimmelman & Assocs.
Client: ABC Television Network

**276**
*Editorial*
Artist: **Merrill Cason**
Art Director: Merrill Cason

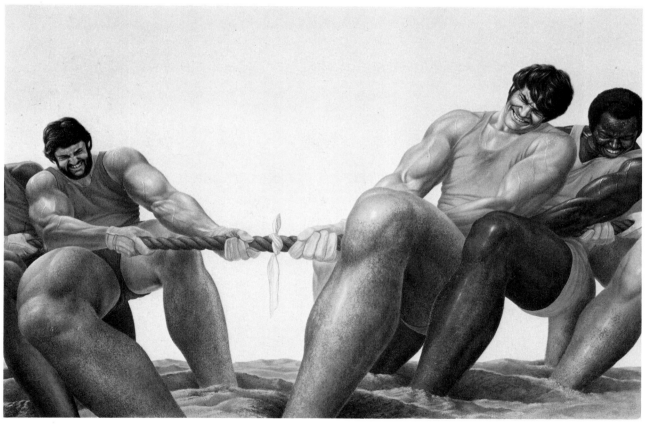

**277**
*Editorial*
Artist: **Eraldo Carugati**
Art Director: Arthur Paul/Len Willis
Publication: Playboy Magazine

274
*Institutional*
Artist: **Alan E. Cober**
Art Director: Nick Kirilloff
Client: National Parks Service

One of Morgan's sharpshooters
possibly Tim. Murphy
· fired the shot
that mortally wounded Fraser.

B. Arnold

**272**
*Editorial*
Artist: **Christopher Spollen**
Art Director: Joseph Connolly
Publication: Genesis Magazine

**273**
*Advertising*
Artist: **Robert Heindel**
Art Director: Stevan Dohanos
Client: The Hartford Insurance Co.

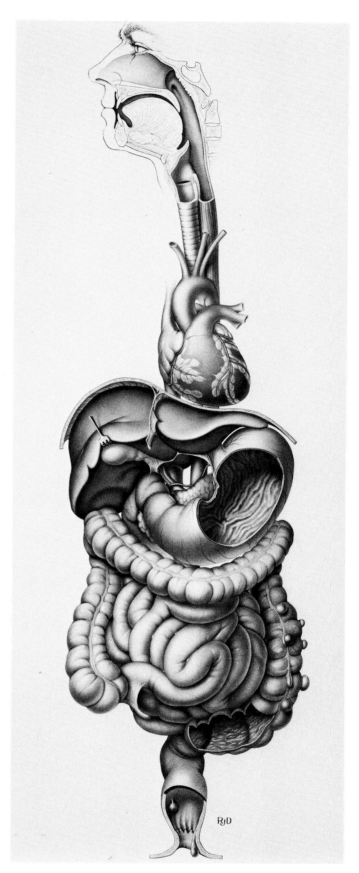

**270**
*Book*
Artist: **Robert LoGrippo**
Art Director: Stephanie Stiles
Title: Windows On Our World: Who Are We?
Publisher: Houghton Mifflin Co.

**271**
*Advertising*
Artist: **Robert J. Demarest**
Art Director: Lawrence Faber
Agency: Medical Conference Inc.
Client: Reed & Carnrick, Inc.

**268**
*Advertising*
Artist: **Stan Hunter**
Art Director: Arthur Ludwig
Agency: Sudler & Hennessey, Inc.
Client: Baxter-Travenol Laboratories

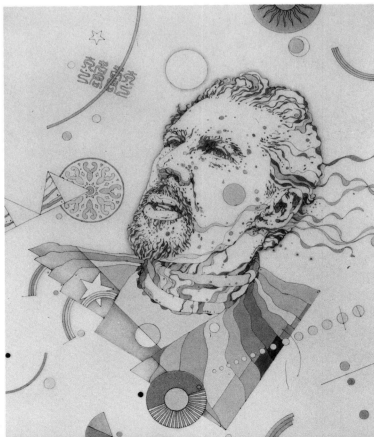

**269**
*Editorial*
Artist: **Terry Steadham**
Art Director: Tom Gould
Publication: Psychology Today Magazine

**266**
*Editorial*
Artist: **Hodges Soileau**
Art Director: John Weaver
Publication: Houston Natural Gas Magazine

**267**
*Institutional*
Artist: **Robert T. Handville**
Art Director: Robert T. Handville
Client: Artists Associates

265
*Editorial*
Artist: **Edward Sorel**
Art Director: K. Francis Tanabe
Publication: The Washington Post

**264**
*Editorial*
Artist: **Robert M. Cunningham**
Art Director: Robert Hallock
Publication: Lithopinion

**262**
*Editorial*
Artist: **Mercer Mayer**
Art Director: Joe Brooks
Publication: Penthouse Magazine

**263**
*Institutional*
Artist: **Gloria Singer**
Art Director: Gloria Singer
Agency: Nu-Line Advertising

315
*Institutional*
Artist: **Don Weller**
Art Director: Don Weller
Agency: The Weller Institute
Client: Triangle Litho

**312**
*Book*
Artist: **Leo & Diane Dillon**
Art Director: Bob Cheney
Title: Deathbird Stories
Publisher: Harper & Row Publishers, Inc.

**313**
*Book*
Artist: **Wendell Minor**
Art Director: Frank Metz
Title: Willard And His Bowling Trophies
Publisher: Simon & Schuster, Inc.

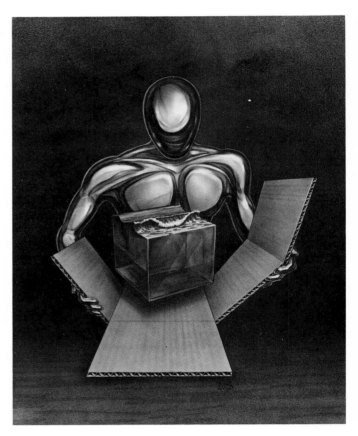

**314**
*Advertising*
Artist: **Roger Huyssen**
Art Director: Samuel N. Antupit
Agency: Antupit & Others
Client: Great Northern Paper Co.

**321**
*Editorial*
Artist: **Tom Wilson**
Art Director: K. Francis Tanabe
Publication: The Washington Post

**322**
*Book*
Artist: **Brad Holland**
Art Director: Frances McCullough
Title: The Geek
Publisher: Harper & Row Publishers, Inc.

**323**
*Editorial*
Artist: **Bernard Fuchs**
Art Director: Robert Hallock
Publication: Lithopinion

**324**
*Editorial*
Artist: **Bernard Fuchs**
Art Director: Robert Hallock
Publication: Lithopinion

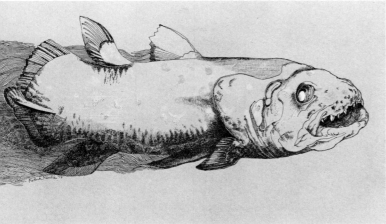

326
*Advertising*
Artist: **Judy Clifford**
Art Director: Steven Jacobs
Agency: Steven Jacobs Design
Client: Simpson Lee Paper Co.

325
*Institutional*
Artist: **Frank Renlie**
Art Director: Frank Renlie

327
*Editorial*
Artist: **David Plourde**
Art Director: James W. O'Bryan
Publication: National Review

**328**
*Editorial*
Artist: **Paul Giovanopoulos**
Art Director: Paul Giovanopoulos

**329**
*Book*
Artist: **Diane Dawson**
Art Director: Diane Dawson

**Fifty Years of Sports Cars**

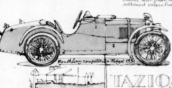

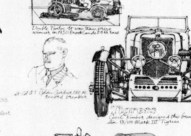

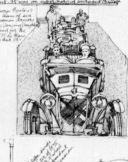

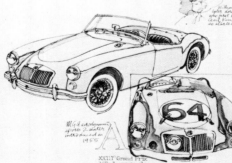

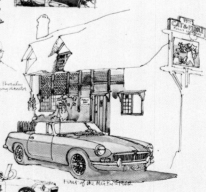

Ken Dalison 1974

The 1933 K3 Magnette supercharged with the cowling concealing the Marshal blower. note the big SU peeking through.

MG K3

**330**
*Advertising*
Artist: **Ken Dallison**
Art Director: John Dugdale
Client: British Leyland Motors, Inc.

**331**
*Institutional*
Artist: **George S. Gaadt**
Art Director: George S. Gaadt

**332**
*Advertising*
Artist: **David Willardson**
Art Director: Bob Versandi
Agency: Gaynor & Ducas
Client: Union Camp Paper

**333**
*Book*
Artist: **Chet Jezierski**
Art Director: Char Lappan
Title: Fawn
Publisher: Little, Brown & Co.

334
*Institutional*
Artist: **Walt Spitzmiller**
Art Director: Walt Spitzmiller
Client: Keeler/Morris Printing Co.

335
*Editorial*
Artist: **Donald M. Hedin**
Art Director: Ira Silberlicht/Tom Lennon
Publication: Emergency Medicine

# WILDERNESS MEDICINE

By John Blosser, M.D.

In the wilderness, as anywhere else, the best way to handle an emergency is to prevent it. So my first piece of advice would be: *Don't go* if you have any kind of medical condition that could cause you trouble. Certainly no one with chronic kidney or lung or heart disease should ever go anyplace where he could be a few days or even just a day away from expert medical care.

For the rest, the first preventive measure is to choose the right clothing for whatever out-of-doors you're going to be in. To begin at the bottom, you'll need good/*continued*

**What do monsters do every midnight?**
They take a coffin break.
**Which is heavier, a half moon or a full moon?**
A half moon, because a full moon is lighter.
**What does the spook who guards the cemetery say
when it hears a strange noise?**
Halt! Who ghost there?
**Why is there always a fence around a cemetery?**
Because so many people are dying to get in.
**How many people are buried in a town cemetery?**
All of them.

**336**
*Book*
Artist: **Reynold Ruffins**
Art Director: Jane Zalben
Title: 1976 Monster Riddle Calendar
Publisher: Charles Scribner's Sons

**337**
*Editorial*
Artist: **Fred Otnes**
Art Director: Charles O. Hyman
Publication: National Geographic

Entertainment

JOIN OR DIE

**338**
*Institutional*
Artist: **Naiad Einsel**
Art Director: Naiad Einsel
Client: National Parks Service

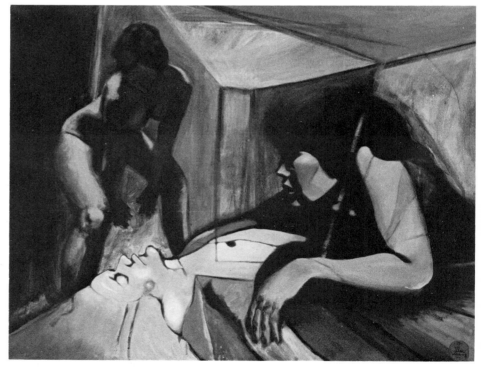

**339**
*Editorial*
Artist: **Glen Weisberg**
Art Director: Glen Weisberg

340
*Editorial*
Artist: **Alex Gnidziejko**
Art Director: Joe Brooks
Publication: Penthouse Magazine

341
*Editorial*
Artist: **David Grove**
Art Director: Gene Butera
Publication: Car & Driver Magazine

**342**
*Institutional*
Artist: **Jim Spanfeller**
Art Director: Joel Siegel
Agency: Hydra

**343**
*Editorial*
Artist: **Paul Williams**
Art Director: Paul Williams

**344**
*Editorial*
Artist: **Sandy Huffaker**
Art Director: Richard Gangel
Publication: Sports Illustrated

**345**
*Advertising*
Artist: **Bernie Karlin**
Art Director: Ace Lehman
Client: RCA Records

**346**
*Editorial*
Artist: **John Berkey**
Art Director: John Berkey

**347**
*Editorial*
Artist: **John Berkey**
Art Director: John Berkey

**348**
*Institutional*
Artist: **Ruth Brunner-Strosser**
Art Director: Ruth Brunner-Strosser

**349**
*Institutional*
Artist: **Ruth Brunner-Strosser**
Art Director: Ruth Brunner-Strosser

**350**
*Book*
Artist: **Robert Shore**
Art Director: David Glixon
Title: An Outcast of the Islands
        by Joseph Conrad (ltd. 2000 copies)
Publisher: Limited Edition Club, Avon, CT ©1975

**351**
*Advertising*
Artist: **Robert Heindel**
Art Director: Joel Snyder
Agency: Doubleday & Co., Inc.
Client: Contempo

OF PETER PROUD

by Max Ehrlich

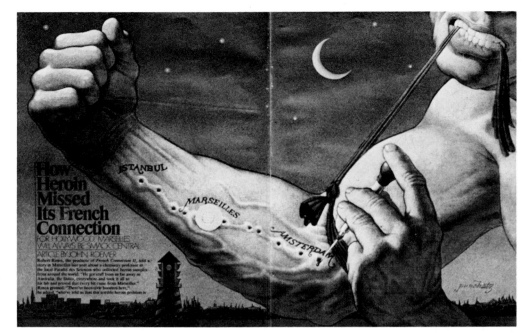

352
*Editorial*
Artist: **Don Ivan Punchatz**
Art Director: Jean-Pierre Holley
Publication: Oui Magazine

353
*Editorial*
Artist: **Wilson McLean**
Art Director: George Kenton
Publication: Oui Magazine
**Award for Excellence**

**354**
*Advertising*
Artist: **C. Royd Crosthwaite**
Art Director: C. Royd Crosthwaite

**355**
*Institutional*
Artist: **Abe Echevarria**
Art Director: Abe Echevarria
**Gold Medal**

**356**
*Advertising*
Artist: **Joseph Veno**
Art Director: Joseph Veno

**357**
*Editorial*
Artist: **Lane Yerkes**
Art Director: Joe Brooks
Publication: Penthouse Magazine

**358**
*Book*
Artist: **Mary Ann Sullivan**
Art Director: Ed Shorts
Title: Songs of the Earth
Publisher: Gibson Greeting Cards, Inc.

**359**
*Book*
Artist: **Mary Ann Sullivan**
Art Director: Ed Shorts
Title: Songs of the Earth
Publisher: Gibson Greeting Cards, Inc.

**360**
*Institutional*
Artist: **Derek Grinnell**
Art Direcfor: Derek Grinnell

**361**
*Editorial*
Artist: **Charles Santore**
Art Director: Bruce Danbrot
Publication: Ladies' Home Journal

**362**
*Editorial*
Artist: **Charles Santore**
Art Director: Herb Bleiwiess
Publication: Ladies' Home Journal

**363**
*Advertising*
Artist: **John Berkey**
Art Director: Larry Wattman/Jerry Leopold
Agency: Poppe-Tyson
Client: Otis Elevator Co.

**364**
*Editorial*
Artist: **Shusei Nagaoka**
Art Director: Andrew Kerechuk

**365**
*Book*
Artist: **Jack Tenenzaph**
Art Director: Jack Tenenzaph

**366**
*Book*
Artist: **Carol Wald**
Art Director: Carol Wald

**367**
*Advertising*
Artist: **Gene Szafran**
Art Director: Joseph Stelmach
Client: RCA Records

**368**
*Editorial*
Artist: **Gabriel Csakany**
Art Director: Evelyn Menassa
Publication: Chatelaine Magazine

**369**
*Institutional*
Artist: **Jackie L. W. Geyer**
Art Director: Jackie L. W. Geyer

**370**
*Editorial*
Artist: **Melinda Bordelon**
Art Director: Arthur Paul/Len Willis
Publication: Playboy Magazine

**371**
*Institutional*
Artist: **Dan Long**
Art Director: Dan Long

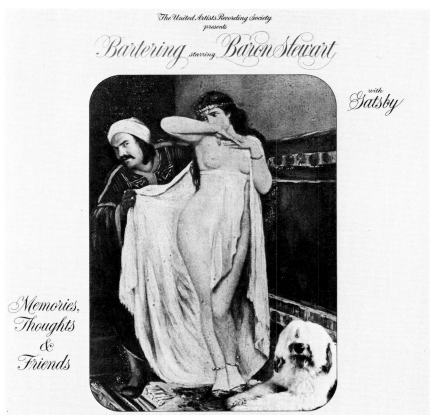

**372**
*Advertising*
Artist: **Bob Cato**
Art Director: Bob Cato
Client: United Artists Records

# AFRICA
## Ceremonial & Folk Music

### Recorded in Uganda, Kenya, and Tanzania
### by David Fanshawe

**374**
*Advertising*
Artist: **Don Brautigam**
Art Director: Paula Bisacca
Agency: The Hub
Client: Nonesuch Records

**373**
*Advertising*
Artist: **Don Brautigam**
Art Director: Paula Bisacca
Agency: The Hub
Client: Nonesuch Records

**375**
*Book*
Artist: **Terry L. Wickart**
Art Director: Terry L. Wickart

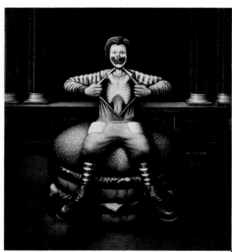

**377**
*Advertising*
Artist: **Charles B. Slackman**
Art Director: John Berg
Client: CBS Records

**376**
*Editorial*
Artist: **David Wilcox**
Art Director: Joe Brooks
Publication: Penthouse Magazine

**378**
*Advertising*
Artist: **Larry Winborg**
Art Director: Larry Winborg
Agency: Winborg & Winborg
Client: Sun Litho

**379**
*Book*
Artist: **Jim Spanfeller**
Art Director: Suzanne Haldane
Title: 4 Way Stop
Publisher: Atheneum

**380**
*Editorial*
Artist: **Jim Spanfeller**
Art Director: Jim Spanfeller

**381**
*Book*
Artist: **Jim Spanfeller**
Art Director: Jim Spanfeller

**382**
*Advertising*
Artist: **Norman MacDonald**
Art Director: Kees de Wyn
Agency: H.V.R.
Client: KLM Royal Dutch Airlines

**383**
*Institutional*
Artist: **Larry Weil**
Art Director: Larry Weil

**384**
*Book*
Artist: **Larry Weil**
Art Director: Larry Weil

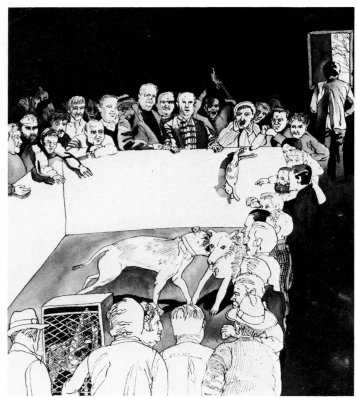

**385**
*Book*
Artist: **Morgan Kane**
Art Director: Ian Summers
Title: Hefner
Publisher: Ballantine Books, Inc.

**386**
*Institutional*
Artist: **Burt Silverman**
Art Director: Burt Silverman
Client: Burt & Claire Silverman

**387**
*Book*
Artist: **Eugene Karlin**
Art Director: James Plumeri
Title: The Other Woman
Publisher: New American Library

**388**
*Book*
Artist: **Gary Kelley**
Art Director: Gary Kelly

**389**
*Institutional*
Artist: **Mark Bellerose**
Art Director: Mark Bellerose

**390**
*Book*
Artist: **Shelley Freshman**
Art Director: Linda Holiday
Title: Cricket
Publisher: Bobbs-Merrill Publishing Co.

**391**
*Institutional*
Artist: **Craig Fetzer**
Art Director: Larry Winborg
Agency: Winborg & Winborg
Client: Bicentennial Graphics

**392**
*Institutional*
Artist: **Andy Buttram**
Art Director: Larry Holland/Andy Buttram
Agency: Wanamaker Advertising Arts
Client: City of Dayton

HILDEBRANDT

**393**
*Book*
Artist: **Gregg & Tim Hildebrandt**
Art Director: Ian Summers
Title: Tolkien Calendar
Publisher: Ballantine Books, Inc.

**394**
*Institutional*
Artist: **Carol Wald**
Art Director: Carol Wald

**395**
*Institutional*
Artist: **Carol Wald**
Art Director: Carol Wald

**397**
*Book*
Artist: **Frances Jetter**
Art Director: Frances Jetter
Title: Growing Up
Publisher: W. Publications

**396**
*Advertising*
Artist: **Roy Carruthers**
Art Director: Elmer Pizzi
Agency: Gray & Rogers
Client: Grit

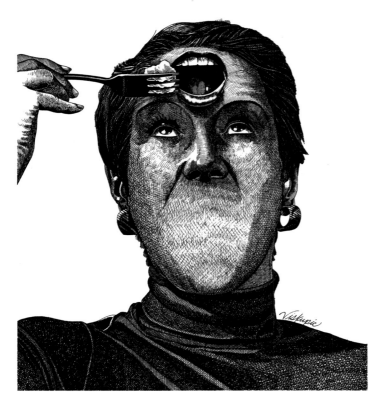

**398**
*Editorial*
Artist: **Gary Viskupic**
Art Director: Cliff Gardiner
Publication: Newsday

**399**
*Book*
Artist: **Phillipe Weisbecker**
Art Director: R. D. Scudellari
Title: Phillip's Chair
Publisher: Random House, Inc.

**400**
*Advertising*
Artist: **John Ryan**
Art Director: John Ryan
Client: CBS-TV

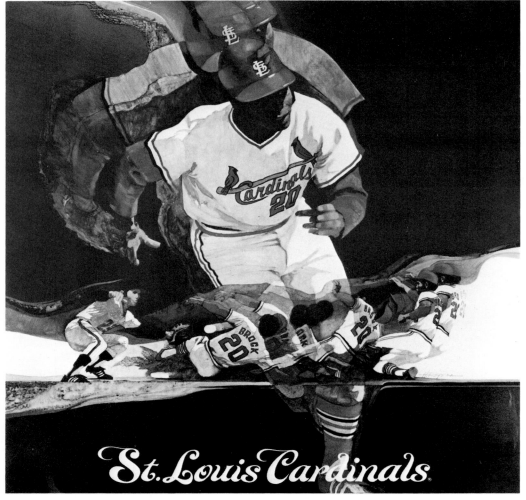

**401**
*Institutional*
Artist: **Howard P. Rogers**
Art Director: Pete Ellebrect
Agency: Gardner Adv. Company
Client: St. Louis Cards

**402**
*Book*
Artist: **Wilson McLean**
Art Director: Ian Summers
Title: Dog Soldiers
Publisher: Ballantine Books

**403**
*Advertising*
Artist: **Richard Sparks**
Art Director: Talivaldis Stubis
Agency: Bill Gold Advertising, Inc.
Client: Universal Pictures

**404**
*Institutional*
Artist: **Robert Cunningham**
Art Director: Harry O. Diamond
Client: Exxon Corporation

**405**
*Editorial*
Artist: **Hiroko Tsuchihashi**
Art Director: Ira Silberlicht/Tom Lennon
Publication: Emergency Medicine

**406**
*Book*
Artist: **Nicholas Gaetano**
Art Director: Barbara Bertoli
Title: Charmed Circle
Publisher: Avon Books

**407**
*Editorial*
Artist: **Ignacio Gomez**
Art Director: Arthur Paul/Bob Post
Publication: Playboy Magazine

**408**
*Advertising*
Artist: **Jim Sharpe**
Art Director: Jim Sharpe

**409**
*Editorial*
Artist: **Robert Grossman**
Art Director: Peter Kleinman
Publication: National Lampoon

**410**
*Advertising*
Artist: **Doug Johnson**
Art Director: Richard Kelly
Agency: Image
Client: West End Brewing Co.

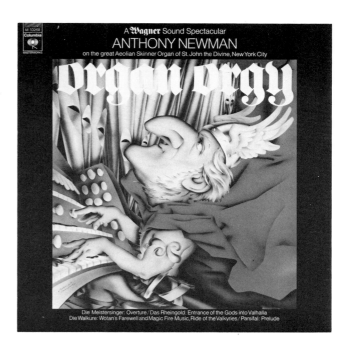

**411**
*Advertising*
Artist: **Robert Grossman**
Art Director: John Berg
Client: CBS Records

**412**
*Book*
Artist: **Leonard B. Lubin**
Art Director: Robert Lowe
Title: The Pig Tail
Publisher: Little, Brown & Co.

**413**
*Book*
Artist: **Leonard B. Lubin**
Art Director: Robert Lowe
Title: The Pig Tail
Publisher: Little, Brown & Co.

**414**
*Editorial*
Artist: **Robert Giusti**
Art Director: Alvin Grossman
Publication: McCall's Magazine
**Award for Excellence**

# IRVING'S DELIGHT
## BY ART BUCHWALD

ROBERT GIUSTI

**Pussy foot** CAT FOOD

**415**
*Editorial*
Artist: **Stan Watts**
Art Director: Peter Kleinman
Publication: National Lampoon

**416**
*Book*
Artist: **Nicholas Brennan**
Art Director: Trelo Bicknell
Title: Olaf's Incredible Machine
Publisher: Windmill Books, Inc.

**417**
*Editorial*
Artist: **Christian Piper**
Art Director: Arthur Paul/Norm Schaefer
Publication: Playboy Magazine

**418**
*Editorial*
Artist: **Charles Shields**
Art Director: Charles Shields

**419**
*Book*
Artist: **Susan Anderson**
Art Director: Barbara Effron
Title: Hodja and the Honored Guest
Publisher: Grolier Incorporated

**420**
*Book*
Artist: **Jerry Pinkney**
Art Director: Harriett Barton
Title: Santeria
Publisher: Atheneum

**421**
*Television*
Artist: **Randall Enos**
Art Director: Dolores Gudzin
Client: National Broadcasting Co.

**422**
*Television*
Artist: **Bob Kurtz**
Art Director: Marilyn Katz/John Swartzwelder
Client: New England Fish Company
**Award for Excellence**

**423**
*Television*
Artist: **Don Weller**
Art Director: Dolores Gudzin
Client: NBC Television Network

**424**
*Television*
Artist: **Ned Levine**
Art Director: Dolores Gudzin
Client: National Broadcasting Co.

**425**
*Book*
Artist: **Ed Lindlof**
Art Director: Richard Hendel
Title: Comic Spirit Of Garcia Lorca
Publisher: University Of Texas Press

**426**
*Institutional*
Artist: **Denis E. Orloff**
Art Director: Lorraine Fox

**427**
*Television*
Artist: **Jerry Karl**
Art Director: Jerry Karl

**428**
*Television*
Artist: **Ed Acuña**
Art Director: Murlin Marsh
Client: NBC Television Network

**429**
*Television*
Artist: **Fred W. Thomas**
Art Director: Dick Paetske
Agency: McCann-Erickson, Inc.
Client: Governor's Committee for the Handicapped

**430**
*Television*
Artist: **Fred W. Thomas**
Art Director: Richard Paetske
Agency: McCann-Erickson, Inc.
Client: Governor's Committee for the Handicapped

**432**
*Editorial*
Artist: **Judith Woodruff**
Art Director: Judith Woodruff

**431**
*Editorial*
Artist: **Peter Lloyd**
Art Director: Arthur Paul/Len Willis
Publication: Playboy Magazine

**433**
*Editorial*
Artist: **Richard Sparks**
Art Director: Joseph Connolly
Publication: Genesis

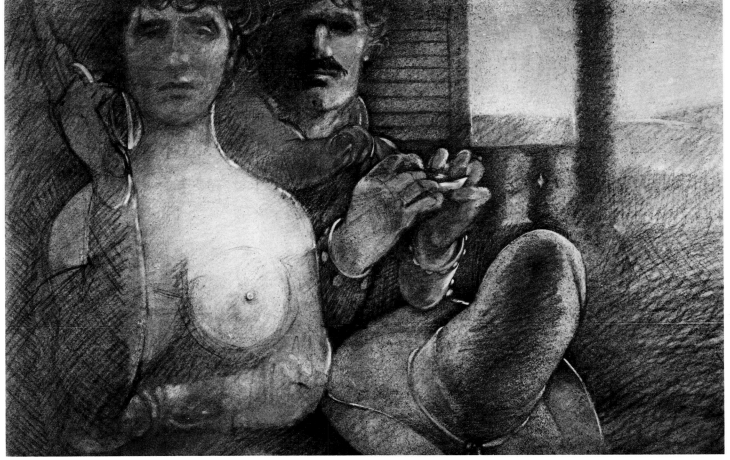

**434**
*Institutional*
Artist: **Walt Spitzmiller**
Art Director: Carolyn Lamont/Henry Epstein
Agency: ABC, Inc.
Client: WABC Sales Development

**435**
*Book*
Artist: **Steve Karchin**
Art Director: Barbara Bertoli
Title: How Many Miles To Babylon
Publisher: Avon Books

**436**
*Institutional*
Artist: **Jim Sharpe**
Art Director: Jim Sharpe

**437**
*Book*
Artist: **Jim Sharpe**
Art Director: Gene Light
Title: Starlight Rider
Publisher: Warner Communications

**438**
*Advertising*
Artist: **Emanuel Schongut**
Art Director: Bob Feldgus
Client: Scholastic Book Services

**439**
*Institutional*
Artist: **Rodica Prato**
Art Director: Rodica Prato

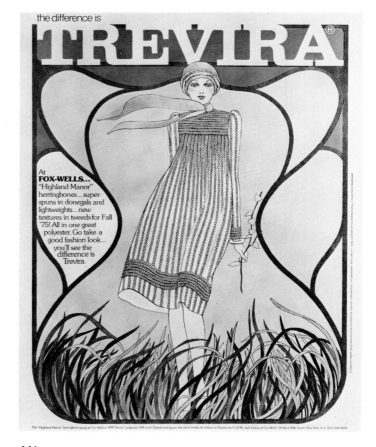

**440**
*Advertising*
Artist: **Thea Kliros**
Art Director: Sal Verne
Agency: Pistone & Verne
Client: Hoechst Fibers Ind.

**441**
*Advertising*
Artist: **Thea Kliros**
Art Director: Sal Verne
Agency: Pistone & Verne
Client: Hoechst Fibers Ind.

**442**
*Advertising*
Artist: **Kaaren Shandroff**
Art Director: Lillian Studer
Agency: Lillian Studer
Client: Lillian Studer

**443**
*Advertising*
Artist: **Bob Pepper**
Art Director: Carl Anderson
Agency: Essie Pinsker Assoc., Inc.
Client: Cranston Print Works Company

**444**
*Advertising*
Artist: **Isadore Seltzer**
Art Director: Ken Brozan
Client: Copco, Inc.

**445**
*Institutional*
Artist: **Fred Otnes**
Art Director: Harry O. Diamond
Client: Exxon Corporation

**446**
*Institutional*
Artist: **Mejo Okon**
Art Director: Mejo Okon

**447**
*Editorial*
Artist: **Richard Ely**
Art Director: Richard Ely

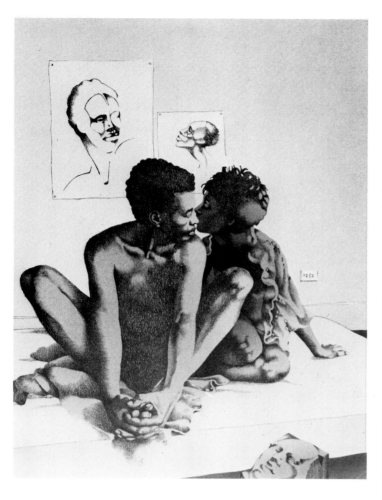

**448**
*Editorial*
Artist: **Nicholas Gaetano**
Art Director: Nicholas Gaetano

**449**
*Book*
Artist: **James Barkley**
Art Director: Lucy Fehr
Title: The Women and the Men
Publisher: William Morrow & Company, Inc.

**450**
*Institutional*
Artist: **Terrell Mashaw**
Art Director: Terrell Mashaw

**451**
*Editorial*
Artist: **Wilson McLean**
Art Director: David Merrill
Publication: Time Magazine
**Award for Excellence**

**452**
*Editorial*
Artist: **Larry Noble**
Art Director: Mino Busi
Publication: Argosy Magazine

**453**
*Advertising*
Artist: **Wally Neibart**
Art Director: Ed Letven
Agency: Ed Letven Assoc.
Client: Berm Studios

**454**
*Editorial*
Artist: **Rick McCollum**
Art Director: Ron Vareltzis/John DeCesare
Publication: Geigy Pharmaceuticals

**455**
*Institutional*
Artist: **Hiroko Tsuchihashi**
Art Director: Hiroko Tsuchihashi
Client: Adwell Audio-Visual Co.

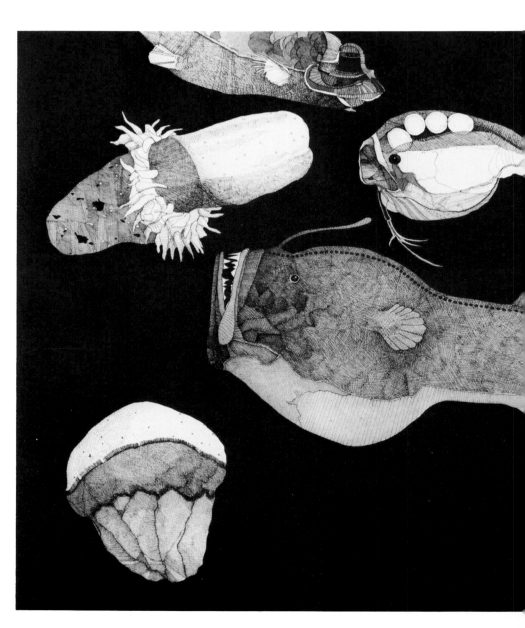

**456**
*Institutional*
Artist: **Erik Sundgaard**
Art Director: Erik Sundgaard

**457**
*Institutional*
Artist: **Koojah Kim**
Art Director: John Fitzer
Client: American Greetings Corp.

**458**
*Institutional*
Artist: **Norman Green**
Art Director: Jerry Anton
Client: Jerry Anton

**459**
*Book*
Artist: **Ezra Jack Keats**
Art Director: Ava Weiss
Title: Louie
Publisher: Greenwillow Books

**460**
*Institutional*
Artist: **Naiad Einsel**
Art Director: Howard Munce
Client: Westport Bicentennial Committee

**461**
*Institutional*
Artist: **Stanley Meltzoff**
Art Director: Thomas S. Ruzicka
Client: American Telephone & Telegraph Co.

**462**
*Institutional*
Artist: **Walt Spitzmiller**
Art Director: Walt Spitzmiller
Client: Keeler/Morris Printing Co.

**463**
*Book*
Artist: **Nancy Yarnall Martin**
Art Director: Nancy Yarnall Martin

**464**
*Editorial*
Artist: **Murray Tinkelman**
Art Director: Ira Silberlicht/Tom Lennon
Publication: Emergency Medicine

**465**
*Institutional*
Artist: **Glen Weisberg**
Art Director: Glen Weisberg

**466**
*Advertising*
Artist: **Bill Shields**
Art Director: Vince Maiello
Agency: Doubleday & Co.
Client: The Literary Guild

**467**
*Institutional*
Artist: **Mike Durbin**
Art Director: Barbara Duff
Client: Houston Grand Opera

ing the battle on Oct 7
at Saratoga
Benedict Arnold
ode onto the
eld and though
e had no
ommand, led
n assault that
used the Germans
join the general
treat into the
albaries Redoubt.

Despite being under
tremendous fire, with
a few men he actually
entered the works,
but his horse was
killed and Arnold
was badly wounded in
the leg.

Alan E. Cober - 73

**468**
*Book*
Artist: **Alan E. Cober**
Art Director: Nick Kirilloff/Vince Gleason
Title: Saratoga
Publisher: National Parks Service

**469**
*Book*
Artist: **Alan E. Cober**
Art Director: Nick Kirilloff/Vince Gleason
Title: Saratoga
Publisher: National Parks Service

**470**
*Book*
Artist: **Rosekrans Hoffman**
Art Director: Constance Berlinger
Title: Kindergarten Social Studies Activity Sheet
Publisher: Houghton Mifflin Co.

**471**
*Book*
Artist: **Frederick Schneider**
Art Director: Frederick Schneider
**Award For Excellence**

**472**
*Editorial*
Artist: **Claudia Karabaic**
Art Director: Lorraine Fox/Marty Minch

**473**
*Book*
Artist: **Sal Barracca**
Art Director: Zlata Paces
Title: Tracks (Solo Book Series R)
Publisher: Macmillan Publishing Co., Inc.

**474**
*Editorial*
Artist: **George Stavrinos**
Art Director: Harry Costas Coulianos
Publication: Gentlemen's Quarterly

**475**
*Editorial*
Artist: **George Stavrinos**
Art Director: Harry Costas Coulianos
Publication: Gentlemen's Quarterly

**476**
*Book*
Artist: **Frank Rakoncey**
Art Director: W. Dobias/A. de Simone
Title: Psychic Powers: Fact or Fraud?
Publisher: The World Book Year Book
Field Enterprises Edu. Corp.

**477**
*Institutional*
Artist: **Lou Brooks**
Art Director: Lou Brooks
Client: Kramer, Miller, Lomden, Glassman

**478**
*Editorial*
Artist: **Larry Noble**
Art Director: John Weaver
Publication: Houston Natural Gas

**479**
*Advertising*
Artist: **Bart Forbes**
Art Director: Andrew Issacson
Agency: Gaynor & Ducas Advertising
Client: Union Camp Paper Co.

**480**
*Television*
Artist: **John Sovjani**
Art Director: Betty Hamilton
Client: NBC Television Network

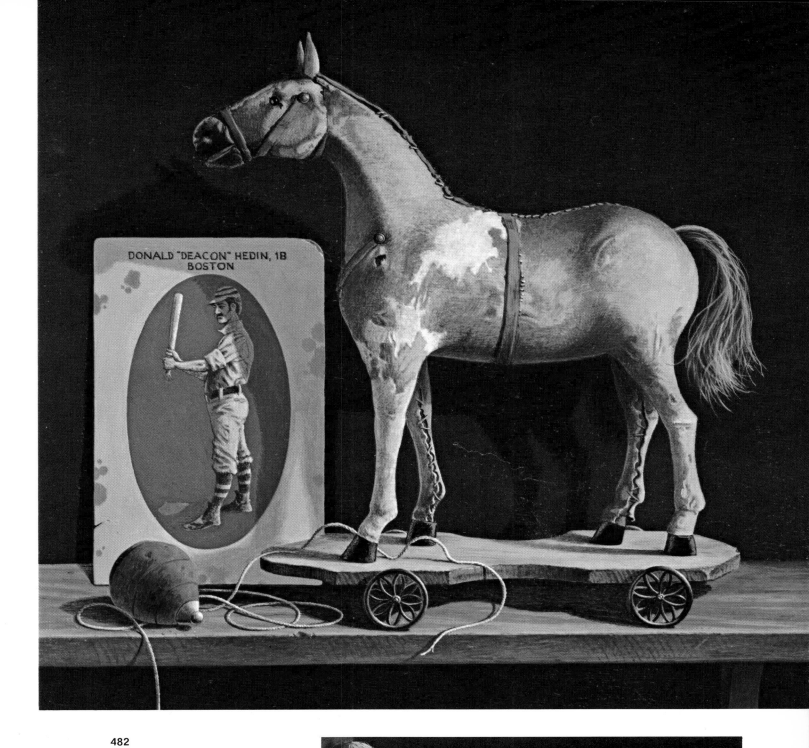

**482**
*Editorial*
Artist: **Donald M. Hedin**
Art Director: Ira Silberlicht/Tom Lennon
Publication: Emergency Medicine

**481**
*Editorial*
Artist: **Dickran Palulian**
Art Director: Leo F. McCarthy
Publication: Swank Magazine

**483**
*Editorial*
Artist: **Gerry Hoover**
Art Director: Harry Costas Coulianos
Publication: Gentlemen's Quarterly

**484**
*Book*
Artist: **Keith Batcheller**
Art Director: Keith Batcheller

**485**
*Institutional*
Artist: **Bart Forbes**
Art Director: Greg Wilder
Client: Sun Graphics

**486**
*Book*
Artist: **Jerry L. Cosgrove**
Art Director: James Plumeri
Title: American Folk Medicine
Publisher: New American Library

**487**
*Advertising*
Artist: **Elizabeth Koda-Callan**
Art Director: Elizabeth Koda-Callan

**488**
*Book*
Artist: **Robert Giusti**
Art Director: Bob Reed
Title: In A Bluebird's Eye
Publisher: Holt, Rinehart & Winston, Inc.

**489**
*Television:*
Artist: **Gerald McConnell**
Art Director: Gerald McConnell

**490**
*Institutional*
Artist: **Gerald McConnell**
Art Director: Howard Munce
Client: Van Nostrand Reinhold Co.

**491**
*Advertising*
Artist: **Charles Santore**
Art Director: Mike Iacobucci
Agency: Gray & Rogers
Client: SPS — Hallowell Div.

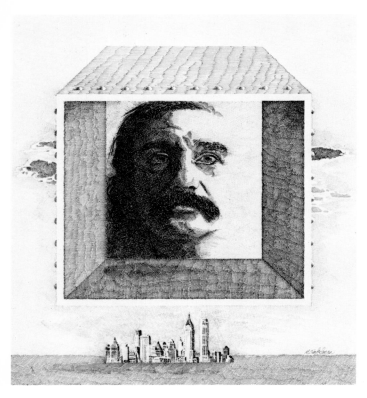

**492**
*Book*
Artist: **Murray Tinkelman**
Art Director: Ian Summers
Title: Dying Inside
Publisher: Ballantine Books, Inc.

**493**
*Book*
Artist: **Murray Tinkelman**
Art Director: Murray Tinkelman

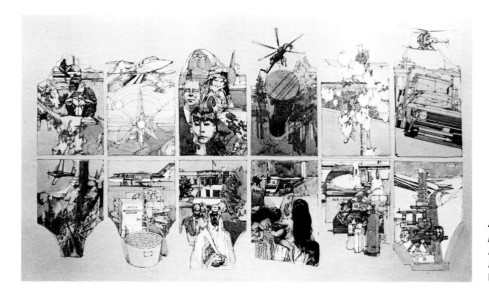

**494**
*Editorial*
Artist: **Barron Storey**
Art Director: Elaine Jones
Publication: Business and Commercial Aviation

**495**
*Institutional*
Artist: **Jerry L. Cosgrove**
Art Director: B. Martin Pedersen
Agency: Pedersen Design, Inc.
Client: Pastimes Publications Inc.

He listened with three ears.
How terrible, how terrible!

How terrible, how terrible!

Brana one day
Rubbed him away
With his eraser.
How terrible, how terrible!

– Dusan Radovic

a poem by a child from Yugoslavia

213

**496**
*Book*
Artist: **Sue Thompson**
Art Director: Jane Olson
Title: HMRS: *Passports*
Publisher: Houghton Mifflin Company

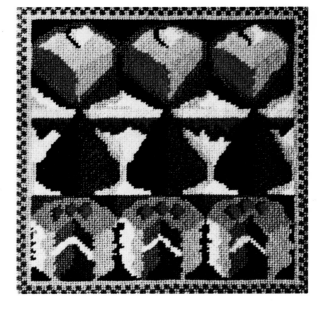

**497**
*Book*
Artist: **Marjorie Sablow/Ralph Miolla**
Art Director: Ralph Miolla
Title: The Jell-o Pudding Sampler
Publisher: General Foods Corp.-Design Center

**498**
*Editorial*
Artist: **Saul Lambert**
Art Director: Richard Gangel
Publication: Sports Illustrated

# ILLUSTRATORS 18

## INDEX

While every effort has been made to insure the accuracy of the credits in this volume, it is inevitable that an occasional error may have crept in. On behalf of the Society of Illustrators, the publishers would appreciate any information about any omissions or corrections. As this book is printed in process colors, we regret that the original colors of some of the illustrations reproduced here have been altered.

## ILLUSTRATORS

Acuna, Ed, 428
462 Riverside Avenue
Westport, CT

Ambrus, Victor G., 205
c/o Oxford University Press
37 Dover Street
London, England

Anderson, Roy H., 154
2 Apricot Lane
Ridgefield, CT

Anderson, Susan, 419
c/o Publishers Graphics
611 Riverside Avenue
Westport, CT 06880

Aristovulos, Nick, 307
16 East 30 Street
New York City

Barensfeld, Mark, 282
7616 LBJ Suite 333
Dallas, TX

Barkley, James, 449
25 Brook Manor
Pleasantville, NY

Barracca, Sal, 473
3635 Island Road
Wantaugh, NY

Baskin, Leonard, 119
c/o The Viking Press
625 Madison Avenue
New York City

Bass, Marilyn, 79
RD 3 Gipsy Trail Road
Carmel, NY

Batcheller, Keith, 484
436 North LaBreda
West Covina, CA

Bellerose, Mark, 31, 90, 389
275 Newbury Street
Boston, MA

Bergman, Barbara, 70
241 East 18 Street
New York City

Berkey, John, 15, 317, 346, 347, 363
c/o Frank & Jeff Lavaty
45 East 51 Street
New York City

Berzofsky, Len, 206, 207
c/o ABC-TV
2040 Broadway
New York City

Bober, Richard, 292
503 Spencer Street
Elizabeth, NJ

Bonner, Lee, 259
2613 Maryland Avenue
Baltimore, MD

Bordelon, Melinda, 370
138 Mountain Road
Cornwall-on-Hudson, NY

Brautigam, Don, 373, 374
29 Cona Court
Haledon, NJ

Brennan, Nicholas, 416
c/o Kestrel Books
17 Grosvenor Gardens
London, England

Brooks, Lou, 477
c/o Kramer, Miller, Lomden,
    Glassman
1528 Waverly Street
Philadelphia, PA

Brown, Charley, 78
Route 1, Box 90
Trinidad, CA

Brunner-Strosser, Ruth, 348, 349
120 North Balph Avenue
Pittsburgh, PA

Buttram, Andy, 392
325 Graceland Drive
West Carrollton, OH

Burd, Robert, 214
409 Warwick Road
Haddonfield, NJ

Calaustro, Braulio, Jr., 118
1255 Anderson Avenue #4
Fort Lee, NJ

Campbell, Jim, 278
c/o Joe Mendola
366 Madison Avenue
New York City

Carruthers, Roy, 208, 396
13 Center Street
Old Greenwich, CT

Carugati, Eraldo, 277
c/o Stephens, Biondia,
Decicco, Inc.
230 East Ohio
Chicago, IL

Cason, Merrill, 276
341 East 87 Street
New York City

Cato, Bob, 372
c/o United Artists Records
6920 Sunset Boulevard
Los Angeles, CA

Chambers, Bill, 30, 209, 210
1607 South Harvard
Arlington Heights, IL

Chaplin, Carl, 116, 226
3757 Eton
Burnaby, British Columbia, Canada

Ciardiello, Joe, 198, 199
25 Charter Oak Road
Staten Island, NY

Clifford, Judy, 169, 326
145 Lark Lane
Mill Valley, CA

Cober, Alan E., 98, 99, 227, 274,
    468, 469
Croton Dam Road
Ossining, NY

CoConis, Ted, 254, 255, 256, 257,
    303
145 East 69 Street
New York City

Collier, John, 286, 287
North Quaker Road
Pawling, NY

Conahan, Jim, 27
1954 North Holbrook Lane
Hoffman Estates, IL

Condak, Clifford, 136, 253
Moffet Road
Cold Springs, NY

Cooley, Gary, 69
320 West 87 Street
New York City

Corwin, Judith Hoffman, 244
333 East 30 Street
New York City

Cosgrove, Jerry L., 486, 495
206 East 38 Street
New York City

Crosthwaite, C. Royd, 85, 354
c/o Frank & Jeff Lavaty
45 East 51 Street
New York City

Csakany, Gabriel, 368
914 Yonge Street #1608
Toronto, Ontario, Canada

Cunningham, Robert M., 181, 264,
    404
177 Waverly Place
New York City

Dallison, Ken, 330
RR #3 Indian River
Ontario, Canada

Dawson, Diane, 216, 329
165 West End Avenue #20N
New York City

Deigan, Jim, 14
c/o Rainbow Grinder
415 Smithfield Street
Pittsburgh, PA

Della-Piana, Elissa, 42
201 Elm St.
Medford, MA

Demarest, Robert J., 271
55 Carol Court
Glen Rock, NJ

Dewey, Kenneth F., 13
220 Fifth Avenue
New York City

Dillon, Diane & Leo, 89, 233, 312
221 Kane Street
Brooklyn, NY

Domingo, Ray, 133
21347 Ellen Drive
Fairview Park, OH

Drucker, Mort, 155
42 Juneau Boulevard
Woodbury, NY

Duke, Chris, 280
c/o Frank & Jeff Lavaty
45 East 51 Street
New York City

Durbin, Mike, 467
10222 Bassoon
Houston, TX

Ebel, Alex, 67
28 Newport Road
Yonkers, NY

Echevarria, Abe, 355
340 10 Street
Brooklyn, NY

Egielski, Richard, 217
7 West 14 Street
New York City

Einsel, Naiad, 338, 460
26 South Morningside Drive
Westport, CT

Einsel, Walter, 74
26 South Morningside Drive
Westport, CT

Ely, Richard, 447
207 West 86 Street
New York City

Endewelt, Jack, 306
50 Riverside Drive
New York City

English, Mark, 47, 62, 235
6010 Cherokee
Fairway, KS

Enos, Randall, 421
11 Court of Oaks
Westport, CT

Fasolino, Teresa, 219
233 East 21 Street
New York City

Faure, Renée, 63
372 Seventh Street
Atlantic Beach, FL

Fetzer, Craig, 391
1461 Sherman Avenue
Salt Lake City, UT

Fiore, Peter M., 92
296B Grove Street
Lodi, NJ

Forbes, Bart, 479, 485
3626 North Hall
Dallas, TX

Fox, Lorraine, 61
4 Kings Terrace
Great Neck, LI, NY

Fraser, Betty, 137
240 Central Park South
New York City

Freshman, Shelley, 261, 390
87-10 51 Avenue
Elmhurst, NY

Fuchs, Bernard, 4, 5, 170, 323,
324
3 Tanglewood Lane
Westport, CT

Gaadt, George S., 331
430 Beaver Street
Sewickley, PA

Gaetano, Nicholas, 11, 252
406, 448
364 East 69 Street
New York City

Gallardo, Gervasio, 121, 236
c/o Frank & Jeff Lavaty
45 East 51 Street
New York City

Garris, Philip, 164
1437 North Poinsettia Place #E
Hollywood, CA

Gersten, Gerry, 212
138 Riverside Drive
New York City

Geyer, Jackie L. W., 369
312 Princeton Avenue
Pittsburgh, PA

Giovanopoulos, Paul, 6, 45, 46,
300, 328
119 Prince Street
New York City

Giusti, Robert, 414, 488
350 East 52 Street
New York City

Glaser, Milton, 120
54 St. Marks Place
New York City

Gnidziejko, Alex, 68, 101, 239, 340
37 Alexander Avenue
Madison, NJ

Gobé, Marc, 49
170 Lombard Street
San Francisco, CA

Goldman, Marvin, 79
RD 3 Gipsy Trail Road
Carmel, NY

Goldsmith, Bill, 241
300 East 59 Street
New York City

Gomez, Ignacio, 407
2657 Locksley Place
Los Angeles, CA

Green, Norman, 458
295 Madison Avenue
New York City

Greer, Bill, 55
RFD 2
Enosberg Falls, VT

Grinnell, Derek, 360
110 North Bayly Avenue
Louisville, KY

Grossman, Robert, 91, 409, 411
19 Crosby Street
New York City

Groth, John, 126
61 East 57 Street
New York City

Grove, David, 341
405 Union Street
San Francisco, CA

Guzzi, George, 22
11 Randlett Park
West Newton, MA

Handville, Robert T., 267
99 Woodland Drive
Pleasantville, NY

Harvey, Dick, 84, 185, 201
119 Florida Hill Road
Ridgefield, CT

Hedin, Donald M., 335, 482
390 Riverside Drive
New York City

Heindel, Robert, 8, 9, 10, 179, 189,
273, 351
Banks Road — Route 1
Fairfield, CT

Hess, Richard, 195
217 East 49 Street
New York City

Hildebrandt, Gregg & Tim, 393
Jackson Avenue
Gladstone, NJ

Ho, Tien, 106, 107, 108
26 Gramercy Park South
New York City

Hobbie, Holly, 25
1300 West 78 Street
Cleveland, OH

Hoffman, Rosekrans, 470
c/o Kirchoff/Wohlberg, Inc.
331 East 50 Street
New York City

Hofmann, William, 65
424 Greenwich
New York City

Holland, Brad, 19, 158, 163, 318,
322 .
96 Green Street
New York City

Holmstrom, Gralyn, 182
c/o Jane Lander Associates
333 East 30 Street
New York City

Hoover, Gerry, 483
c/o Kirchoff/Wohlberg, Inc.
331 East 50 Street
New York City

Huens, Jean Leon, 220, 221
c/o Frank & Jeff Lavaty
45 East 51 Street
New York City

Huffaker, Sandy, 93, 344
67 East 11 Street
New York City

Hunter, Stan, 268
c/o Frank & Jeff Lavaty
45 East 51 Street
New York City

Huyssen, Roger, 51, 103, 314
345 East 81 Street
New York City

Inouye, Carol, 105
134 West 88 Street
New York City

Isom, Joe, 200, 247, 248
10047 Lamar
Overland Park, KS

Jampel, Judith, 21, 39, 43, 279
148 Columbus Avenue
New York City

Jarvis, David, 283
924 Westwood Boulevard
Los Angeles, CA

Jean, Carole, 58
45 Oriole Drive
Roslyn, NY

Jetter, Frances, 397
57 Montague Street
Brooklyn, NY

Jezierski, Chet, 81, 333
c/o Frank & Jeff Lavaty
45 East 51 Street
New York City

Johnson, Doug, 16, 29, 410
20 East 17 Street
New York City

Kalish, Lionel, 291
55 East 86 Street
New York City

Karabaic, Claudia, 472
99-33 42 Avenue
Corona, NY

Karchin, Steve, 54, 435
80 Irving Place
New York City

Karl, Jerry, 427
1045 Eglon Court
North Merrick, NY

Karlin, Bernie, 345
A.K.M. Studios
41 East 42 Street
New York City

Karlin, Eugene, 387
39-73 48 Street
Sunnyside, NY

Kane, Morgan, 385
500 East 77 Street
New York City

Keats, Ezra Jack, 459
444 East 82 Street
New York City

Kelley, Gary, 82, 83, 388
c/o Hellman Design Association
126 Leland
Waterloo, IA

Kilmer, David, 224
1009 Timberlea Drive
Palatine, IL

Kim, Koojah, 457
129 Guimida Lane #6
Anaheim, CA

Kliros, Thea, 440, 441
130 West 3 Street
New York City

Koda-Callan, Elizabeth, 487
792 Columbus Avenue
New York City

Kohfield, Dick 153
1 Walter Avenue #15
Norwalk, CT

Koslow, Howard, 80
26 Highwood Road
East Norwich, CT

Kriss, Ronald D., 134, 211
1816 Redcliff Street
Los Angeles, CA

Kurtz, Bob, 422
1724½ North Whitley Avenue
Hollywood, CA

Lambert, Saul, 498
153 Carter Road
Princeton, NJ

Lapsley, Robert E., 180
2037 Norfolk
Houston, TX

Lawrence, Vint, 38
3221 Macomb Street, NW
Washington, DC

Levine, David, 156, 157
1 Pierre Pont Street
Brooklyn, NY

Levine, Ned, 424
657 Nassau Road
Uniondale, NY

Lewis, Maurice, 175
2402 Tangley
Houston, TX

Lindlof, Ed, 20, 425
2103 Travis Heights Boulevard
Austin, TX

Llerena, Carlos Antonio, 17
110 Sullivan Street #1B
New York City

Lloyd, Peter, 71, 290, 431
11049 Blix Street
North Hollywood, CA

LoGrippo, Robert, 26, 270
1200 Beacon Hill Drive
Dobbs Ferry, NY

Long, Dan, 190, 371
c/o Jane Lander Associates
333 East 30 Street
New York City

Lowery, Robert S., 130
419 West 56 Street
New York City

Lubin, Leonard B., 412, 413
367 6 Street
Brooklyn, NY

Luczak, Dennis, 64, 109, 316
160 Florida Hill Road
Ridgefield, CT

Macdonald, Holland S., 288
2946 Quinlan Street
Yorktown Heights, NY

MacDonald, Norman, 382
Herenstraat 29
Voorhout, The Netherlands

Mack, Stan, 173
45 Easterwood Avenue
Dobbs Ferry, NY

Maffia, Daniel, 86, 138
70 Grand Avenue
Engelwood, NJ

Magee, Alan, 72, 75
RD 2 Swamp Road
Newtown, CT

Martin, Nancy Yarnall, 463
2264 Marlon Avenue
Pennsauken, NJ

Mashaw Terrell, 450
2700 Boll
Dallas, TX

Mayer, Mercer, 262
Route 67
Roxbury, CT

McCance, Lew, 125
Box 583
Georgetown, CT

McCollum, Rick, 454
5 Palmieri Lane
Westport, CT

McConnell, Gerald, 302, 489, 490
8 East 23 Street
New York City

McGinnis, Robert E., 113
30 Meadowbank Road
Old Greenwich, CT

McIntosh, Jon, 281
33 Marlborough Street
Boston, MA

McKissick, Randall, 73
5917 McBride Street
Charlotte, NC

McLean, Wilson, 123, 183, 223,
353, 402, 451
70 East 56 Street
New York City

McMahon, Franklin, 202
155 North Mayflower Road
Lake Forest, IL

McPhail, David, 23
c/o Stone Soup
315 Cambridge Street
Boston, MA

McVicker, Charles, 37
505 Prospect Avenue
Princeton, NJ

Melia, Paul, 311
3030 Regent Street
Dayton, OH

Meltzoff, Stanley, 461
126 Grange Avenue
Fair Haven, NJ

Meyrowitz, Rick, 232
181 Mott Street
New York City

Minor, Wendell, 129, 191, 313
277 West 4 Street
New York City

Miolla, Ralph, 497
c/o General Foods
250 N Street
White Plains, NY

Miyauchi, Haruo, 213
207 East 32 Street
New York City

Moss, Donald, 122
78 Haights Cross Road
Chappaqua, NY

Moss, Geoffrey, 18, 162
315 East 68 Street
New York City

Mulatier, Jean, 237
Paris, France

Nagaoka, Shusei, 53, 364
400 South Hauser Boulevard #10K
Los Angeles, CA

Nakai, Michael, 33
202 Riverside Drive
New York City

Neibart, Wally, 453
1715 Walnut Street
Philadelphia, PA

Newton, Richard F., 222
9450 North Keeler Avenue
Skokie, IL

Noble, Larry, 278, 452
6526 Pinehurst
Houston, TX

Nordbok, AB, 112
Foreningsgatan 34
Goteborg, Sweden

Ochagavia, Carlos, 40, 41
c/o Frank & Jeff Lavaty
45 East 51 Street
New York City

Okon, Mejo, 446
152 North Franklin Road
Indianapolis, IN

Oni, 104
3514 Tulip Drive
Yorktown Heights, NY

Orloff, Denis E., 426
7 West 14 Street
New York City

Otnes, Fred, 171, 172, 296, 297,
337, 445
Chalburn Road
West Redding, CT

Ovies, Joseph M., 225
17280 Nadora
Southfield, MI

Palladini, David, 2, 56, 141, 184
60 Riverside Drive
New York City

Palulian, Dickran, 139, 481
18 McKinley Street
Rowayton, CT

Parker, Robert Andrew, 192, 193,
240
c/o Ted Riley
252 East 49 Street
New York City

Peak, Bob, 124, 196, 299
70 East 56 Street
New York City

Pepper, Bob 443
157 Clinton Street
Brooklyn, NY

Pinkney, Jerry, 167, 168, 420
41 Furnace Dock Road
Croton-on-Hudson, NY

Piper, Christian, 417
487 Broadway #1201
New York City

Plourde, David, 327
Mountainside Road
Warwick, NY

Podwil, Jerry, 301
108 West 14 Street
New York City

Prato, Rodica, 439
c/o Jane Lander Associates
333 East 30 Street
New York City

Punchatz, Don Ivan 140, 352
2021 South Cooper
Arlington, TX

Quay, Steve & Tim, 194
718 South Sixth Street
Philadelphia, PA

Rakoncey, Frank, 476
7615 North Kildare
Skokie, IL

Rand, Ted, 97
1417 Fourth Avenue
Seattle, WA

Reinhard, Siegbert, 142, 143, 144,
145
3682 Barham Boulevard
Los Angeles, CA

Renlie, Frank, 325
500 Aurora North #204
Seattle, WA

Rogers, Howard P., 401
Cobbs Mill Road
Weston, CT

Rosenblatt, Lee, 305
c/o The National Lampoon
635 Madison Avenue
New York City

Ruffins, Reynold, 336
38 East 21 Street
New York City

Ryan, John, 400
4225 64 Street
Woodside, NY

Sablow, Marjorie, 497
143 Darling Avenue
New Rochelle, NY

Saldutti, Denise, 215
33 Stratford Drive
Colonia, NJ

Samuels, Ed, 238
103 The Bowery
New York City

Santore, Charles, 231, 361, 362,
491
138 South 20 Street
Philadelphia, PA

Saris, Anthony, 150
103 East 86 Street
New York City

Schaare, Harry J., 310
1921 Valentines Road
Westbury, NY

Schleinkofer, David, 161
60 Forest Lane
Levittown, PA

Schneider, Frederick, 471
1 Hudson Street
New York City

Schongut, Emanuel, 438
Box 247
Mountaindale, NY

Schorr, Todd, 319
1517 Lombard Street
Philadelphia, PA

Schrier, Jeffrey A., 3, 320
71 West 85 Street #3A
New York City

Schwartz, Daniel, 127, 228, 289,
298
118 East 28 Street #901
New York City

Seltzer, Isadore, 444
70 East 56 Street
New York City

Sandroff, Kaaren, 442
992 Richard Court
Teaneck, NJ

Sharpe, Jim, 284, 285, 408, 436,
437
5 Side Hill Road
Weatport, CT

Shields, Charles, 165, 418
3051 Richmond Boulevard
Oakland, CA

Shields, Bill, 466
2003 Franklyn Street
San Francisco, CA

Shore, Robert, 178, 350
218 Madison Avenue
New York City

Silverman, Burt, 386
324 West 71 Street
New York City

Singer, Gloria, 263
2306 Ocean Avenue
Brooklyn, NY

Slackman, Charles B., 87, 377
400 East 57 Street
New York City

Smith, Mavis, 76
243 Ryerson Street #602
Brooklyn, NY

Smith, Philip, 117
5592 Ranchers Way
Carmichael, CA

Soesenbeth, Volker, 94, 95
Spelmansbacken 15
Spånga, Sweden

Soileau, Hodges, 266
5116 Morningside
Houston, TX

Sorel, Ed, 131, 265
Cold Spring Road
Carmel, NY

Sovjani, John, 44, 66, 102, 480
1867 Glenrock Street
Yorktown Heights, NY

Soyka, Ed, 159, 166
15 South Buckhout Street
Irvington, NY

Spanfeller, Jim, 342, 379, 380, 381
Mustato Road
Katonah, NY

Sparks, Richard, 1, 308, 403, 433
12 Burlington Drive
Norwalk, Ct

Spitzmiller, Walt, 260, 334, 434,
462
88 Lyons Plain Road
Weston, CT

Spollen, Christopher J., 251, 272
41 Groton Street
Staten Island, NY

Sposato, John, 218
43 East 22 Street
New York City

Spunbuggy Works, Inc., 50
8506 Sunset Boulevard
Los Angeles, CA

Stavrinos, George, 474, 475
207 East 32 Street
New York City

Steadham, Terry, 57, 269
3601 North Pennsylvania
Indianapolis, IN

Storey, Barron, 128, 197, 242, 243,
494
c/o Jane Lander Associates
333 East 30 Street
New York City

Sullivan, Mary Ann, 358, 359
5 East Lake Shore #30
Cincinnati, OH

Sumichrast, Jözef, 135, 258
535 North Michigan Avenue #1116
Chicago, IL

Sundgaard, Erik, 203, 204, 456
821 Cornwall Avenue
Cheshire, CT

Szafran, Gene, 77, 367
c/o Artists Associates
211 East 51 Street
New York City

Tauss, Herb, 229
South Mountain Pass
Garrison, NY

Templeton, Sandra M., 34
1814 South Vermont #6
Independence, MO

Tenenzaph, Jack, 365
123-40 83 Avenue
Queens, NY

Terpning, Howard, 115
RD #7 Goodridge Road
Redding, CT

Thomas, Fred W., 177, 429, 430
1823 Terry
Seattle, WA

Thompson, Dean, 88
10931 Bloomfield
North Hollywood, CA

Thompson, John M., 186, 187
171 Duane Street
New York City

Thompson, Sue, 496
Honeyhill Road RD #3
Georgetown, CT

Tinkelman, Murray, 12, 174, 464,
492, 493
75 Lakeview Avenue West
Peekskill, NY

Tople, Larry, 293
c/o Art Morat
4947 Cimarron
Bloomfield Hills, MI

Towle, Faith M., 111
128 Match A Mary
Chanakyopuri
New Delhi, India

Tsuchihashi, Hiroko, 405, 455
153 East 26 Street
New York City

Unruh, Jack, 249
333 7616 LBJ
Dallas, TX

Upshur, Thomas, 132
20 Perarsal Place
Roslyn Heights, LI, NY

Vaeth, Susan, 96
59 East 75 Street
New York City

Vallejo, Boris, 250
24 St. Andrews Place
Yonkers, NY

VanNutt, Robert, 188
194 West 10 Street
New York City

Velthuijs, Max, 309
Nord-Sud Verlag
8617 Monchaltorf, Switzerland

Veno, Joseph, 356
246 Commonwealth Avenue
Boston, MA

Ventura, Piero, 294, 295
Via Domenichino, 27
20149 Milan, Italy

Viskupic, Gary, 36, 398
7 Westfield Drive
Centerport, LI, NY

Visser, Lucas R., 304
488 East Floyd Drive
Sandy, UT

Wald, Carol, 366, 394, 395
182 Grand Street
New York City

Watts, Stan, 415
c/o Sketch Pad Studio
2021 East South Cooper
Arlington, TX

Weil, Larry, 383, 384
421 East 81 Street
New York City

Weisbecker, Phillipe, 399
1 Rue des Dardanelles
Paris, France

Weisberg, Glen, 339, 465
315 East 70 Street
New York City

Welkis, Allen M., 100
53 Heights Road
F. Salonga, NY

Weller, Don, 28, 110, 246, 315,
423
340 Mavis Drive
Los Angeles, CA

Whitesides, Kim, 52
c/o Rabin & Winborn
135 East 54 Street
New York City

Wickart, Terry L., 375
O.S. 613 East Street
Winfield, IL 60190

Wilcox, David, 160, 376
163 Montclaire Avenue
Montclaire, NJ

Wilkes, Gene, 152
1148 Briarcliff Road
Atlanta, GA

Wilkes, Tom, 230
1722 Whitley Avenue
Hollywood, CA

Willardson, David, 332
2224 Ponet Drive
Los Angeles, CA

Williams, Michael Kelly, 176
5202 Commonwealth
Detroit, MI

Williams, Paul, 343
c/o Frank & Jeff Lavaty
45 East 51 Street
New York City

Willson, Richard, 35
Shepherds Hill
Peaslake, Surrey, England

Wilson, Reagan, 7, 151
43 Avery Drive NE
Atlanta, GA

Wilson, Tom, 321
2028 P Street NW
Washington, DC

Winborg, Larry, 378
141 Pierpont
Salt Lake City, UT

Winborn, Marsha, 24
822 Queen Anne Avenue #16
Seattle, WA

Wolfe, Bruce, 245
206 El Cerrito Avenue
Piedmont, CA

Woodruff, Judith, 432
321 North Martel Avenue
Los Angeles, CA

Yerkes, Lane, 234, 357
85 East Plumstead Avenue
Lansdowne, PA

Yohe, Tom, 48, 275
c/o McCaffrey & McCall
575 Lexington Avenue
New York City

Ziel, George, 114
225 East 47 Street
New York City

Ziemienski, Dennis, 59, 60
244 Emerson Street
Palo Alto, CA

## ART DIRECTORS

Adair, Jim, 40
Altholz, Cathy, 251
Amft, Robert, 222
Anderson, Betty, 194
Anderson, Carl, 443
Anderson, Roy H., 154
Anthony, Carolyn, 129
Anton, Jerry, 458
Antupit, Samuel N., 98, 99, 173,
314

Back, Paul, 36
Barensfeld, Mark, 282
Bartels, David, 245
Barton, Harriett, 420
Bass, Marilyn, 79
Batcheller, Keith, 484
Behar, Linda, 31
Bellerose, Mark, 90, 389
Berg, John, 131, 136, 193, 238,
253, 377, 411
Berkey, John, 346, 347
Berlinger, Constance, 470
Bertoli, Barbara, 70, 71, 113, 406,
435
Berzofsky, Len, 206, 207
Bicknell, Trelo, 416
Bisacca, Paula, 373, 374
Blanco, Steven, 255, 303
Bleiweiss, Herb, 62, 235, 362
Bonner, Jim, 4, 5
Bradford, John, 104
Bratman, Jack, 179
Brent, Michael, 156, 188
Brocker, Nick, 247
Brodkin, Ed, 317
Brooks, Joe, 77, 109, 139, 262, 340
357, 376
Brooks, Lou, 477
Browning, Orval, 24
Brozan, Ken, 444
Brunner-Strosser, Ruth, 348, 349
Burke, E. A., 44
Busi, Mino, 452
Butera, Gene, 341
Buttram, Andy, 392
Byrd, Robert, 214

Cadge, William, 286, 287, 298
Calaustro, Braulio, Jr., 118
Carpenter, Robert, 110
Cason, Merrill, 276
Cato, Bob, 164, 372
Cencora, Ed, 13
Chambers, Bill, 30, 209, 210
Charles, Milton, 75, 80, 159
Cheney, Bob, 312
Chwast, Seymour, 213
Ciardiello, Joe, 198, 199
Cipriani, Robert, 31
Clarke, Grace, 294, 295
Clemente, Tom, 296
Condak, Henrietta, 131, 136
Conner, Al, 63
Connolly, Joseph, 272, 433
Contreras, Gerry, 76, 92
Coulianos, Harry Costas, 2, 474,
475, 483
Cox, Linda, 183, 257, 291, 292
Crosthwaite, C. Royd, 85, 354
Csatari, Joe, 61, 150

Danbrot, Bruce, 361
David, Michael, 16
Davis, Marion, 105, 115
Dawson, Diane, 216, 329
DeCesare, John, 170, 454
de Simone, A., 476
de Wyn, Kees, 382
Diamond, Harry O., 112, 192, 404,
445
Dobians, W., 476
Dohanos, Steven, 273
Dougherty, Robert M., 69, 103
Duff, Barbara, 467
Dugdale, John, 330
Duke, Chris, 280

Echevarria, Abe, 355
Effron, Barbara, 419
Egielski, Richard, 217
Einsel, Naiad, 338
Einsel, Walter, 74
Ellebrect, Pete, 401
Ely, Richard, 447
Epstein, Henry, 434
Erlanger, Richard, 17

Faber, Lawrence, 271
Falcon, Dave, 187
Fazio, Joe, 47, 121
Fehr, Lucy, 218, 449
Feitler, Bea, 219
Feldgus, Bob, 308, 438
Ferrara, Lidia, 26, 86, 157
Fishbach, Lee, 114
Fisher, Gordon, 8, 9, 10
Fitzer, John, 457
Fox, Lorraine, 426, 472

Gaadt, George S., 32, 331
Gaetano, Nicholas, 11, 448
Gangel, Richard, 91, 122, 127,
202, 344, 498
Gardiner, Cliff, 398
Gavin, Robert, 89
Geyer, Jackie L. W., 369
Giovanopoulos, Paul, 300, 328
Gleason, Vince, 468, 469
Glixon, David, 350
Glusker, Irwin, 45, 46, 65, 125,
189

Gobé, Marc, 49
Goldman, Marvin, 79
Goodman, Alan, 123
Gould, Thomas, 78, 134, 211, 269
Green, Jerry, 116
Gregory, William, 306
Grinnell, Derek, 360
Grossman, Alvin, 414
Grumm, Fred, 15
Gudzin, Dolores, 55, 278, 421,
423, 424
Guzzi, George, 22

Haldane, Suzanne, 379
Hallek, Graham, 116
Hallock, Robert, 227, 264, 323,
324
Hamilton, Betty, 58, 480
Handville, Robert T., 267
Harridsloff, Ed, 52
Hedden, Jim, 133
Heller, Steve, 19, 21
Hendel, Richard, 425
Hess, Richard, 195
Hinden, Stan, 18
Hinshaw, Kirk, 59
Ho, Tien, 106, 107, 108
Holiday, Linda, 261, 307, 390
Holland, Larry, 392
Holley, Jean-Pierre, 84, 140, 352
Holmstrom, Gralyn, 182
Huig, Max, 63
Hutcheson, Harold, 175
Hyman, Charles, 171, 337

Iacobucci, Mike, 491
Innes, David Ford, 50
Issacson, Andrew, 479

Jacobs, Steven, 169, 326
Jampel, Judith, 279
Jetter, Frances, 397
Johnson, Doug, 16
Johnson, Rowan, 316
Jones, Elaine, 494
Jordan, Ken, 170, 252

Karl, Jerry, 427
Katz, Marilyn, 422
Kelley, Chuck, 152
Kelley, Gary, 82, 83, 388
Kelly, Richard, 410
Kennedy, Paul, 98, 99
Kenton, George, 353
Kerechuk, Andrew, 364
Kingsbury, Robert, 212
Kirilloff, Nick, 274, 468, 469
Kleinman, Peter, 232, 305, 409,
415
Klemin, Diana, 230
Koda-Callan, Elizabeth, 487
Kohfield, Dick, 153
Kowalski, Ray, 25
Krackehl, Gene, 96
Kravec, Joseph, 14

Lamont, Carolyn, 434
Landa, Peter, 168
Lappan, Char, 191, 333
Lapsley, Robert E., 180
Lazzarotti, Salvatore, 201
Lee, Ed, 290
Lehman, Ace, 345
Lennon, Tom, 166, 335, 405, 464,
482
Lenox, George, 20

Leone, Leonard, 229
Leopold, Jerry, 363
Letven, Ed, 453
Levitt, Herbert, 223
Light, Gene, 437
Long, Dan, 190, 371
Long, Larry, 42
Lorraine, Walter, 111
Loscocco, Nicholas, 22
Lowe, Robert, 23, 412, 413
Lowery, Robert S., 130
Lubalin, Herb, 174
Ludwig, Arthur, 268

Macdonald, Holland S., 288
Magee, Alan, 72
Maiello, Vince, 172, 260, 466
Marsh, Murlin, 54, 66, 102, 428
Martin, Nancy Yarnall, 463
Mashaw, Terrell, 450
McCarthy, Leo F., 141, 184, 197, 481
McConnell, Gerald, 302, 489
McCullough, Frances, 163, 318, 322
McIntosh, Jon, 281
McKissick, Randall, 73
McVicker, Charles, 37
Melia, Paul, 311
Menassa, Evelyn, 368
Menell, Don, 68, 101, 239
Merrill, David, 155, 246, 284, 285, 451
Metz, Frank, 313
Minch, Marty, 472
Miolla, Ralph, 497
Moran, Lynne, 296
Morat, Art, 293
Mortensen, Gordon, 301
Moss, Geoffrey, 18, 162
Moxcey, Ralph, 167
Moy, George, 316
Munce, Howard, 460, 490

Noble, Louise, 241
Noring, Soren, 45, 46, 65, 189, 228
Nowak, Bob, 41

O'Bryan, James W., 327
Okon, Mejo, 446
Olson, Jane, 496
Ong, James, 208
Ovies, Joseph M., 225

Paces, Zlata, 33, 137, 473
Paetske, Dick, 429, 430
Paine, Howard E., 220, 221
Patchowsky, Borys, 161
Patterson, Brenda, 176
Paul, Arthur, 67, 87, 158, 277, 301, 370, 407, 417, 431
Pedersen, B. Martin, 495
Phillips, Steve, 39
Pierson, George, 244
Pihlstroem, Anders, 94, 95
Piper, Richard, 97
Pizzi, Elmer, 236, 237, 396
Plumeri, James, 132, 297, 387, 486
Pollack, Burton, 1
Pope, Kerig, 67, 87, 226
Post, Bob, 158, 407
Powell, Dallas, 224
Prato, Rodica, 439
Pringle, John, 259

Ramp, Irene, 29
Rauch, Peter, 103
Reed, Bob, 488

Reid, Scott, 283
Reinhard, Siegbert, 142, 143, 144, 145
Renlie, Frank, 325
Rooney, Elaine, 181
Ruzicka, Thomas S., 461
Ryan, John, 400

Saldutti, Denise, 215
Schaare, Harry J., 310
Schaefer, Norm, 417
Scher, Paula, 120, 138, 160
Schmidt, Toby, 231
Schneider, Frederick, 471
Schorr, Todd, 319
Schrier, Jeffrey A., 3
Scudellari, Bob, 86, 399
Seidman, Eric, 93
Sharpe, Jim, 408, 436
Shields, Charles, 165, 418
Shore, Robert, 178
Shorts, Ed, 358, 359
Siegel, Joel, 342
Silberlicht, Ira, 100, 166, 335, 405, 464, 482
Silverman, Burt, 386
Singer, Gloria, 263
Smith, Philip, 117
Smolen, Don, 124, 196
Snyder, Joel, 351
Solie, John, 51
Sorvino, Skip, 56
Spanfeller, Jim, 380, 381
Spiegelman, Abby, 64
Spitzmiller, Walt, 334, 462
Standley, Linda, 60
Stelmach, Joseph, 185, 367
Stiles, Stephanie, 270
Stockwell, Jo, 200
Stubis, Talivaldis, 254, 299, 403
Studer, Lillian, 442
Sugar, Bert, 289
Sumichrast, Jozef, 135, 258
Summerford, Jack, 249
Summers, Ian, 43, 114, 250, 256, 385, 393, 402, 492
Sundgaard, Erik, 203, 204, 456
Swartzwelder, John, 422
Sweeney, Stan, 81

Tanabe, K. Francis. 35, 38, 265, 321
Tehon, Atha, 240
Templeton, Sandra M., 34
Tenenzaph, Jack, 365
Thomas, Fred W., 177
Thompson, Dean, 88
Thompson, John M., 186
Thrasher, Ed, 320
Tinkelman, Murray, 493
Tsuchihashi, Hiroko, 455, 300

Vareltzis, Ron, 6, 454
Veno, Joseph, 356
Verne, Sal, 440, 441
Versandi, Bob, 332
Victor, Claire, 316
Visser, Lucas R., 304

Wald, Carol, 366, 394, 395
Wattmen, Larry, 363
Weaver, Jessica M., 201
Weil, Larry, 383, 384
Weisberg, Glen, 339, 465
Weiss, Ava, 459

Weller, Don, 28, 315
Westray, Kathleen, 119, 233
Wickart, Terry L., 375
Wilder, Greg, 485
Williams, Paul, 343
Willis, Len, 277, 370, 431
Wilson, Reagan, 7, 151
Winborg, Larry, 378, 391
Winslow, Will, 205, 309
Wise, Guinotte, 248
Wittliff, William, 126
Wolin, Ron, 53
Woodruff, Judith, 432
Wroth, Will, 57

Yerkes, Lane, 234
Yochum, Elmer, 128, 242, 243

Zalben, Jane, 336
Zinn, Richard, 27
Zuckerman, Linda, 233

## TELEVISION ANIMATION DIRECTOR:

Kimmelman, Phil, 48, 275

## TELEVISION PRODUCER

Yoher, Tom, 48, 275

## TELEVISION PRODUCTION AGENCIES

Kimmelman, Phil, & Assocs., 48, 275
McCann-Erickson, Inc., 429, 430
Schöen-Rogers, Inc., 50

## CLIENTS

ABC Television Network, 48, 206, 275
Adwell Audio-Visual Co., 455
American Greetings Corp., 25, 457
American Honda Motor, Inc., 53
American Revolution Bicentennial, 181
American Telephone & Telegraph Co., 461
Anton, Jerry, 458
Aristocrat Printing, Inc., 22
Artists Associates, 267
Atlantic Records, 120, 138, 160

Baxter-Travenol Laboratories, 268
Benson & Hedges, 223
Berm Studios, 453
Bicentennial Graphics, 391
British Leyland Motors, Inc., 330
Broadcast Music, Inc., 41

CBS Records, 131, 136, 193, 238, 253, 290, 377, 411
CBS Television, 51, 400

CKNW Broadcasting, 116
Caedmon Records, 89
Cappac Farms, 186
Chelsea Theatre of Brooklyn, 16
Chemagro, 200
Children's Hospital of Philadelphia, 231
City of Dayton, 392
Commercial Credit, 259
Contempo, 351
Converse Rubber Co., 31
Copco, Inc., 444
Cranston Print Works Co., 443
Curacao Tourist Board, 187

Dayton, City of, 392
Deans Foods Co., 245
Delli, Carpini, Kaylor, Inc. 118
Detroit Diesel Allison, 293

Emergency Medicine, 100
Exxon Corporation, 112, 179, 192, 404, 445

Franklin Typographers, 195

Gagosian, Larry, Prints on Broxton 11
Geigy in House, 121
Geigy Pharmaceuticals, 6, 252
Governor's Committee for the Handicapped, 429, 430
Graftech Corp., 73
Grateful Dead Records, 164
Great Northern Paper Co., 314
Grit, 236, 237, 396

Hartford Insurance Co., The, 273
Hewlett-Packard, 60
Hoechst Fibers Ind., 440, 441
Houston Grand Opera, 467

KLM Royal Dutch Airlines, 382
Keeler/Morris Printing Co., 334, 462
Kramer, Miller, Lomden, Glassman, 477

Lander, Jane, Associates, 182
Literary Guild, The, 172, 260, 466

Male Slacks, 152
McNally-Pittsburg, 248
Merrill, Charles E., Co., 281
Mexican National Tourist Council, 255, 303
Mobil Oil Corp., 125

NBC Television Network, 54, 55, 58 66, 102, 244, 423, 428, 480
National Broadcasting Co., 278, 421, 424
National Guard, 81
National Parks Service, 12, 274, 302, 338
Navy Recruiting Command, 15
New England Fish Co., 422
Nonesuch Records, 373, 374

Oshkosh B'gosh, Inc., 50
Otis Elevator Co., 363

PPG Industries, 14
Pastimes Publications, Inc., 495
Picante Press, 28
Pratt Institute, 92
Push Pin Studios, 213

RCA Records, 185, 345, 367
Rapp, Gerald & Cullen, 143, 145
Reed & Carnrick, Inc., 271
Roberts, Ira, Publishing Co., 142, 144

SPS-Hallowell Div., 491
St. Louis Cards, 401
San Francisco Zoo, 59
Scholastic Book Services, 308, 438
Scholastic Magazine, 56
Scott Paper Co., 128, 222, 242, 243
Shawmut Banks, 42
Shell Oil Co., 175
Silverman, Burt & Claire, 386
Simpson Lee Paper Co., 169, 326
Sonoma Vineyards, 49
Studer, Lillian, 442
Sun Graphics, 485
Sun Litho, 378
Sunrise Publications, Inc., 57
Svenska Pappershandiare-föreningen, 94, 95

Texaco, 13
Tournament of Roses, 58
Triangle Litho, 315
20th Century-Fox, 317

U.S. Air Force, 153
Union Camp Paper, 332, 479
United Artists, 124, 196
United Artists Records, 372
United Graphics, 97
Universal Pictures, 403
University of Utah, 304
Utica National Insurance Group, 123

Van Nostrand-Reinhold Co., 490
Varo, Inc., 249
von Feldman, Dr. Arnold, 74

WABC Eyewitness News, 207
WABC Sales Development, 434
WLS-TV, 208
Warner Brothers, Inc., 133, 254, 299
Warner Brothers Records, 320
Warren Paper, 167
West End Brewing Co., 410
West-Port-Orleans, Ltd., 4, 5
Westport Bicentennial Committee, 460

## PUBLISHERS

Addison-Wesley Publishing Co., 205, 309
Argosy, 289, 452
Atheneum, 379, 420
Avon, Limited Editions Club, 350
Avon Books, 70, 71, 113, 406, 435

Ballantine Books, Inc., 43, 114, 250, 256, 385, 393, 402, 492
Bantam Books, 229
Bobbs-Merrill Publishing Co., 261, 307, 390
Boston Globe, The, 18, 162
Boys Life Magazine, 61, 150
Business and Commercial Aviation, 494

Car & Driver Magazine, 341
Chatelaine Magazine, 368
Childcraft, 27
Cosmopolitan Magazine, 182, 257, 291, 292
Coward, McCann & Geoghegan, Inc., 251

Daily Newspapers of U.S.A. & Canada, 296
Dial Press, The, 240
Doubleday & Co., Inc., 230
Dover Publishing Co., 98, 99

Emergency Medicine, 166, 335, 405, 464, 482
Encino Press, 126

Family Circle, 104
Field Enterprises Edu. Corp., 476
Forum for Contemporary History —Skeptic Magazine, 283
Franklin Library, The, 8, 9, 10

Geigy Pharmaceuticals, 47, 170, 454
General Foods Corp. —Design Center, 497
Genesis Magazine, 272, 433
Gentlemen's Quarterly, 2, 474, 475, 483
Gibson Greeting Cards, Inc., 358, 359
Greenwillow Books, 459
Grolier Incorporated, 419
Guideposts Magazine, 201

Harper & Row Publishers, Inc., 163, 312, 318, 322
Harpers Weekly, 17
Holt, Rinehart & Winston, Inc., 488
Houghton Mufflin Co., 111, 241, 270, 470, 496
Houston Natural Gas Magazine, 266, 278

Imperial International Learning Corp., 24
Institutional Investor Magazine, 156, 188

Jacksonville Magazine, 63

Knopf, Alfred A., 86, 157, 194

Ladies' Home Journal, 62, 235, 361, 362
Limited Editions Club, 350
Lithopinion, 227, 264, 323, 324
Little, Brown & Co., 23, 191, 333, 412, 413

Macmillan Publishing Co., Inc., 33, 79, 137, 473
McCall's Magazine, 414
Money Magazine, 69, 103
Morrow, William, Co., 218, 449
Ms Magazine, 219

National Geographic Magazine, 220, 221, 337
National Geographic Society, 171
National Lampoon, 232, 305, 409, 415
National Parks Service, 468, 469
National Review, 327

New American Library, 132, 297, 387, 486
New Times, 39
New York Times, The, 19, 21, 93
Newsday, 36, 398

Oui Magazine, 68, 84, 101, 140, 239, 352, 353

Patient Care, 1
Penny, J.C., Forum, 173
Penthouse Magazine, 77, 139, 109, 262, 340, 357, 376
Playboy Magazine 67, 87, 158, 226, 277, 301, 370, 407, 417, 431
Playgirl Magazine, 110
Pocket Books, 75, 80, 159
Psychology Today, 78, 134, 211, 269

Random House, Inc., 26, 294, 295, 399
Reader's Digest, The, 45, 46, 65, 105, 115, 189, 228, 306
Redbook, 286, 287, 298
Ronile Press, 178

Scholastic Magazines, 96
Scribner's, Charles, Sons, 336
Simon & Schuster, Inc., 313
Skeptic Magazine, 283
Southern Illinois University Press, 20
Sports Illustrated 91, 122, 127, 202, 344, 498
Stereo Review, 161
Straight Arrow Books, 212
Swank Magazine, 141, 184, 197, 481

Time Magazine, 29, 155, 246, 284, 285, 451

University of Texas Press, 425

Viking Press, The, 119, 233
Viva Magazine, 316

W. Publications, 397
Warne, Frederick, & Co., 168
Warner Communications, 437
Washington Post, The, 35, 38, 265, 321
Wee Wisdom, 247
Weybright & Tailey, 129
Wiley, John & Sons, 44
Windmill Books, Inc., 416
World Book Year Book, The, 476

## AGENCIES

ABC, Inc., 434
Antupit & Others, 314
Aristocrat, Inc., 22

Benton & Bowles, Inc., 13
Bonner, Jim, Adv. Art, 4, 5

Cannon Advertising, Inc., 255, 303
Chermayeff & Geismar Assocs., 181

D'Arcy, MacManus & Masius, 293
Diener Hauser Greenthal Co., Inc., 52, 317

Doner, W. B., & Co., 81, 259
Doubleday & Co., Inc., 172, 351, 466

Foote, Cone & Belding, Inc., 59
Frank, Clinton E., 245

Gardner Adv. Co., 401
Gaynor & Ducas Advertising, 332, 479
Geer DuBois, 40
Geigy Pharmaceuticals, 121
Gold, Bill, Advertising, Inc., 133, 254, 299, 403
Gray & Rogers, Inc., 236, 237, 396, 491
Gregory Fosella Assoc., 42
Grey Advertising, Inc., 15, 53
Gunn Associates, 31

H. V. R., 382
Hub, The, 373, 374
Humphrey, Browning, MacDougal, 167
Hydra, 342

Image, 410

Jacobs, Steven, Design, 169, 326

Kelley, Chuck, Design, 152
Ketchum, MacLeod & Grove, 14, 128, 242, 243

Leber, Katz Partners, 123
Letven, Ed, Assoc., 453

McKim Advertising, 116
McKissick/Illustrator, 73
Medical Conference, Inc., 271
Milea Sinclair, 64

Nu-Line Advertising, 263

Ogilvy & Mather, Inc., 175
Ong & Associates, 208

Pedersen Design, Inc., 495
Performing Dogs, 16
Pinsker, Essie, Assoc., Inc., 443
Pistone & Verne, 440, 441
Poppe-Tyson, 363

Richards Group, 249

Schoenkopf & Westrell AB, 94, 95
Smolen, Smith & Connolly, 124, 196
Studer, Lillian, 442
Sudler & Hennessey, Inc., 268

Tromson, Monroe, 187

United Artists Records, 164
University Design, 304

Valentine/Radford Adv., 200, 248

Wanamaker Advertising Arts, 392
Weller Institute, The, 28, 315
Wells, Rich & Green, 223
Winborg & Winborg, 378, 391

Zakin & Comerford, 41

# ILLUSTRATORS 18

**PRODUCTION CREDITS**
THE TYPE IN THIS BOOK IS Palatino with Helvetica Light and Medium
COMPOSITION BY M. J. Baumwell, Typography
OFFSET PLATES AND PRINTING BY Connecticut Printers, Inc.
THE PAPER IS Mead's Black and White Offset Enamel Dull
PAPER SUPPLIER Andrews/Nelson/Whitehead Publishing Papers
BINDING BY A. Horowitz and Son
JACKET PRINTED BY Princeton Polychrome Press
PRODUCTION SUPERVISION Lee Tobin, Hastings House
ASSISTANT TO THE PUBLISHER James Moore, Hastings House

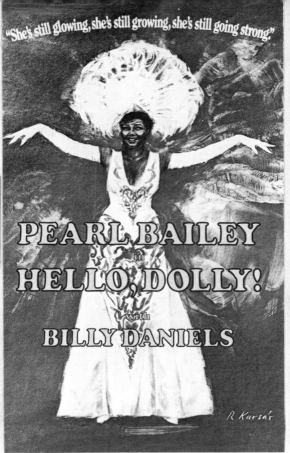
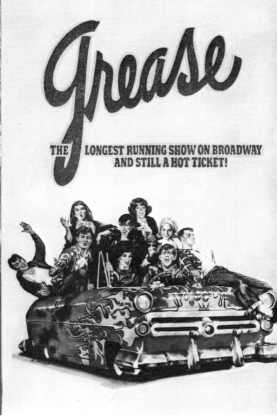

# WHAT IT TAKES TO BE A SUCCESSFUL ARTIST:

1. You must develop a style that is unique and commercial. A style that is artistically excellent and yet able to effectively sell a product or idea.

2. You must have speed and reliability, time after time, no matter what your disposition or the deadline. Remember: you truly are only as good as your last job.

3. You must offer a competitive price. Competitive doesn't mean low. It means fair. Fair to the talents of the artist and fair to the client.

4. You must be a professional at all times. The professional understands the problems of the artist and the marketplace and solves them.

5. You must know the marketplace. Who will buy your art and for how much, and you must always keep expanding and diversifying your markets.

6. You must package and promote your talent. Like any successful product, your style must be presented correctly to the widest possible audience.

7. You must keep up with your field. That means never stop growing and learning. Never become "dated".

8. You must "go beyond the point of discouragement". When things get difficult or uneven, you must have the inner resources to renew yourself.

9. You must have patience. The patience to get the training, experience, testing and judgment that make a successful artist.

10. You must recognize what you, as an artist, can do, and get help in those areas that you cannot handle.

The secrets of the successful artist are the same as for any successful endeavor: talent, hard work, desire, persistence, promotion, outside help, and a little bit of luck. Being an artist can be one of the most rewarding and exciting fields anywhere, and we are proud to be part of it.

Barbara Gordon
Associates Ltd.
165 East 32 Street
New York, N.Y. 10016
212-686-3514

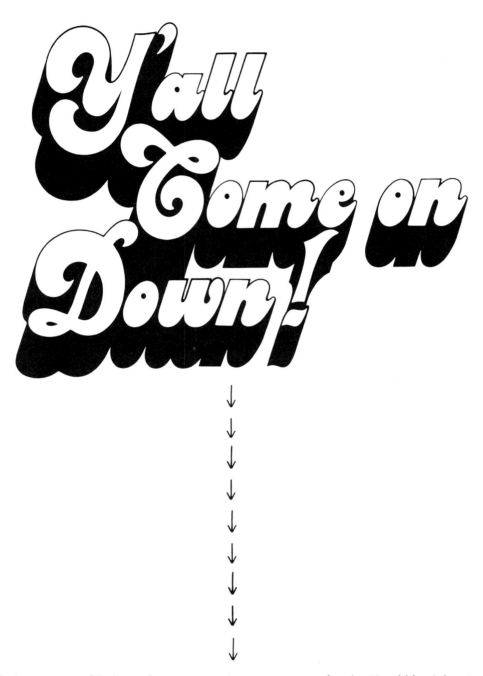

*We hope you'll drop in on us whenever you're in the Washington area. We like visitors, and we'd enjoy showing you our new home.*

*Time-Life Books Inc.*
*777 Duke Street*
*Alexandria, Va. 22314*
*Tel: (703) 960-5200*

# artists

*Norman Adams, David Byrd,
John Collier, Norman La Liberte,
Dennis Luczak, John Martin,
Fred Otnes, Gene Szafran.*

*Represented by:
Bill Erlacher, Artists Associates
211 East 51 Street, New York, N.Y. 10022
Telephone:(212)755-1365/6
Associates: Arlene Reiss,
Madeline Renard*

# The finest Designers' Gouache and Brushes on either side of the Atlantic!

Winsor & Newton Designers' Gouache Colors are world renowned for their versatility and brilliance. The 78 colors of great covering power and unmatched opacity are superior to any poster or ordinary gouache color. First choice of commercial artists and designers everywhere!

Winsor & Newton's Series 7 Pure Red Sable

Brushes are unequalled. Their unsurpassed excellence is attributable to the rigid selection from the many thousands of Kolinsky tails used annually in the production of sable brushes. Imported from England, Winsor & Newton takes infinite pains to provide superb quality to the tip of your brush.

*At your art supply store*

## WINSOR AND NEWTON

555 Winsor Drive, Secaucus, N.J. 07094

Canadian Agents The Hughes Owens Company Ltd Montreal
Northwestern Dist Pacific Stationery Portland Ore

# JESSIE NEELEY

JESSIE NEELEY ARTIST REPRESENTATIVE 575-1234

# art staff inc.

**An Advertising & Design Service**

369 Lexington Ave., New York, N.Y. 10017 • (212) 867-2660

**The name Lavaty has stood behind outstanding art for over 30 years.**

You'll find contemporary and nostalgic styles treating all subjects. Individual portfolios are available from the following artists represented exclusively by Frank and Jeff Lavaty.

John Berkey, Don Daily, Bernard D'Andrea, Roland Descombes, Chris Duke, Gervasio Gallardo, Martin Hoffman, Stan Hunter, Chet Jezierski, Mort Kunstler, Lemuel Line, Robert Logrippo, Charles Moll, Carlos Ochagavia, Robert Schulz.

## Contact Frank & Jeff Lavaty for free color booklet.

Representative booklet of 100 color examples available for your file. Phone (212) 355-0910. Or write Frank and Jeff Lavaty, 45 East 51st St., N.Y., N.Y. 10022.

ART & ILLUSTRATION

ART

FRANK & JEFF LAVATY — ARTIST REPRESENTATIVES
45 EAST 51st STREET, N.Y., N.Y. 22. **PHONE** 212-355-0910

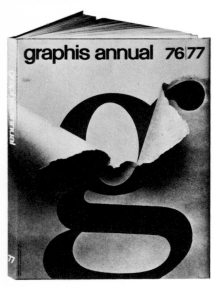

ROY MILLER, JR. ADVERTISING ART

5378 HAZELHURST STREET • PHILADELPHIA, PENNSYLVANIA 19131

SIGNATURE

PITT STUDIOS
1370 ONTARIO STREET
216·241·6720
CLEVELAND · PITTSBURGH

## We're scouting Heavy Hitters

Illustrators with promising batting averages. With big-league potential. With the drive & desire to rate someday with Bernard Fuchs, Bob Peak or Mark English.

Pitt Studios' range of consumer and institutional accounts offers plenty of chances to swing away. We seldom bunt.

Pitt (55 years in Cleveland and Pittsburgh) is the largest studio in our part of the world. We're looking for illustrators who can render line & wash, B&W & color. Make crisp layout indications and finished art. Draw figures well.

Don't wait for our scouts to find you. Send samples (on slides, please) to Carl W. Behl, President, Pitt Studios, 1370 Ontario Street, Cleveland, Ohio 44113. Or phone collect: 216/241-6720.

Run-producers come in any age. But we need illustrators with at least 3 years' experience.

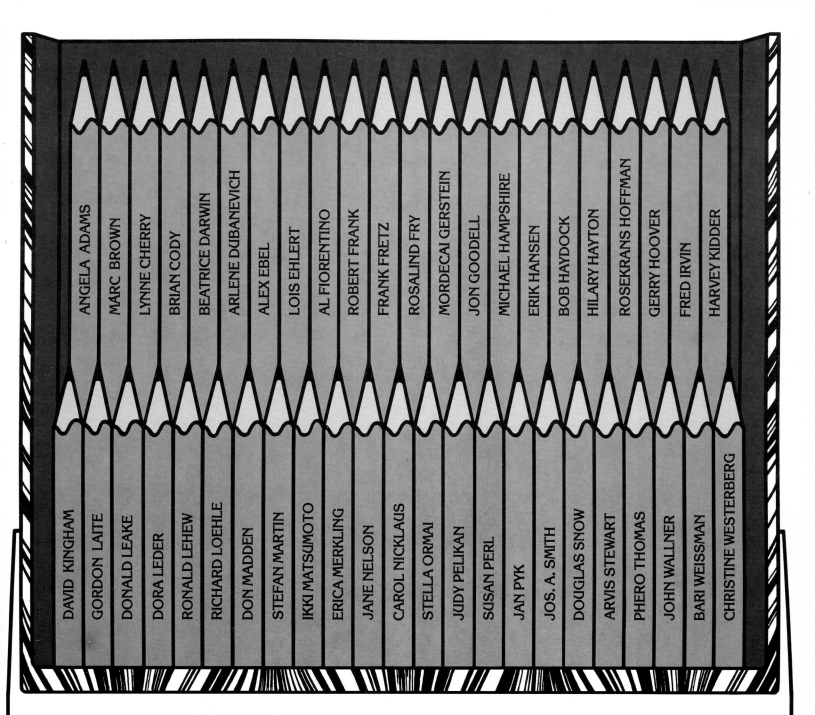

ANGELA ADAMS
MARC BROWN
LYNNE CHERRY
BRIAN CODY
BEATRICE DARWIN
ARLENE DUBANEVICH
ALEX EBEL
LOIS EHLERT
AL FIORENTINO
ROBERT FRANK
FRANK FRETZ
ROSALIND FRY
MORDECAI GERSTEIN
JON GOODELL
MICHAEL HAMPSHIRE
ERIK HANSEN
BOB HAYDOCK
HILARY HAYTON
ROSEKRANS HOFFMAN
GERRY HOOVER
FRED IRVIN
HARVEY KIDDER

DAVID KINGHAM
GORDON LAITE
DONALD LEAKE
DORA LEDER
RONALD LEHEW
RICHARD LOEHLE
DON MADDEN
STEFAN MARTIN
IKKI MATSUMOTO
ERICA MERKLING
JANE NELSON
CAROL NICKLAUS
STELLA ORMAI
JUDY PELIKAN
SUSAN PERL
JAN PYK
JOS. A. SMITH
DOUGLAS SNOW
ARVIS STEWART
PHERO THOMAS
JOHN WALLNER
BARI WEISSMAN
CHRISTINE WESTERBERG

# Kirchoff/Wohlberg, Inc.

## artists representative

433 East 51 Street
New York, New York 10022
212-753-5146

589 Boston Post Road
Madison, Connecticut 06443
203-245-7308

**Learn from us.
And our friends.**

**The people who
buy, sell and create
illustration.**

Six of todays'
great illustrators,
Alan E. Cober,
Mark English,
Bernie Fuchs,
Bob Heindel,
Fred Otnes,
Robert Peak,
and their
distinguished
guests including,
Herb Bleiweiss,
John deCesare,
Harry O.Diamond,
Dick Gangel,
Harvey Kahn,
Dave Merrill,
Susan E. Meyer
Lou Silverstein,
and
Atha Tehon

Alan E. Cober,
Mark English,
Bernie Fuchs,
Bob Heindel,
Fred Otnes, and
Robert Peak

invite you to
attend
**The Illustrators'
Seminar
June 26-July 1**

Learn from us and our guests at this
one-week seminar featuring presen-
tations by The Illustrators, and by top
Art Directors, Designers and Reps.
Every aspect of illustration from concept through corrections will be
covered.

invite you to stay
and attend
**The Illustrators'
Workshop
June 26-July 22**

Following the seminar, this three-
week, limited enrollment workshop,
will feature work critiques, portfolio
evaluation, and daily one-to -one
discussions with The Illustrators. And
live projects will be assigned. A fantas-
tic opportunity for those who qualify.

Come for a week or stay for a month.

For details on where and how much,
write: Michael J. Smollin, Managing
Director

**The Illustrators'
Workshop**

P.O. Box 280, Easton, Conn. 06425
203-938-2355

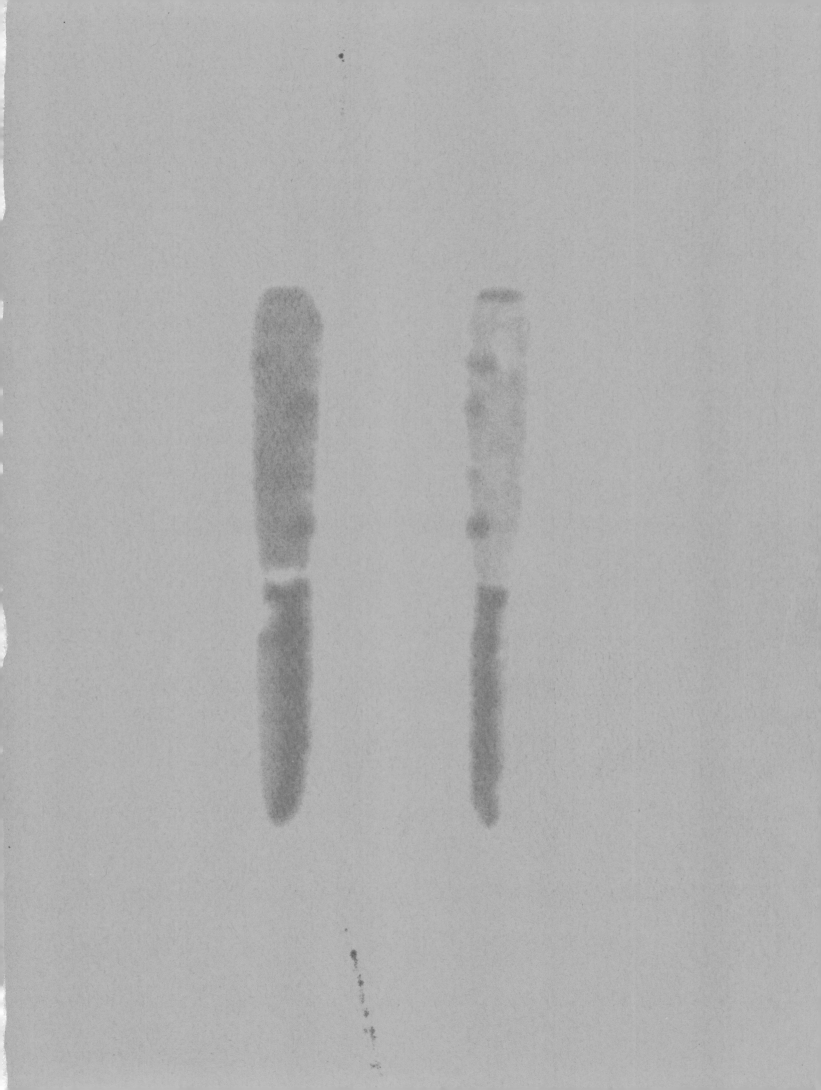